C
Hi

Madhur Gupta is one of the leading Odissi dance
maestros of his generation. *The Indian Express* has
hailed Gupta as one of the few male artists (in a field
mostly dominated by women), who not only pursued
Indian classical dance with devotion but also excelled
at it. Beginning his initial training in Kathak with a
maestro like Padma Vibhushan awardee, Pandit Birju
Maharaj, he was strongly drawn towards Odissi as his
life's calling.

He has also had the fortune of interacting
and learning from masters like Madhavi Mudgal,
Bichitrananda Swain and Kumkum Lal. Madhur is
currently in advanced training under the renowned
dancer and Guru, Smt Sharon Lowen in the Padma
Vibhushan Guru Kelucharan Mohapatra style of Odissi.

Apart from extensively touring, performing and
writing, Madhur also teaches Odissi at Sangeet Vidya
Niketan, New Delhi.

'In this insightful book, Madhur Gupta covers two-and-a-half millennia of history, unfolding the lives of the female courtesans who have sadly been maligned and ignored. Gupta, an accomplished Odissi dancer, strives to repair this injustice, producing a fascinating story in the process.'

—**Dr Shashi Tharoor**
Author, politician and former international civil servant

'Choosing to be an artist has, throughout time, been a brave and radical decision. When the person making that choice is a woman, then the barriers and discrimination women have faced in society in general only serve to multiply the difficulties of an artist's life. Given the circumstances, Madhur's book is a breath of fresh air. A consummate Odissi dancer himself, his understanding and love of the arts informs every story he shares. His book does a great service in undoing the erasure of so many incredible female artists who came before.'

—**Anoushka Shankar**
Sitar player, film composer and activist

'Women have not been given their very much-deserved and due importance historically as well as in the present time in the social structure of India. Throughout Indian history you will find examples of how women led from the front while men failed to do so. I pray that when this book is complete and in circulation, it brings an understanding to one and all of the unparalleled bravery and contribution of women of India, past and present.'

—**Ustad Zakir Hussain**
Tabla player, composer, music producer, percussionist and film actor

'The history of the woman performer in India is the story of intersectionality—of gender, caste, class, religion and region. The glory attached to them, in retrospect, often couches patriarchy and the entitlement of class and caste. Madhur's book is an important step in pulling away some euphemistic veils and digging into their actual stories.'

—**Dr Mallika Sarabhai**
Indian classical dancer, actress and social activist

'I congratulate Madhur wholeheartedly on his most interesting project...'

—**Maestro Zubin Mehta**
Master conductor of western classical music

Courting Hindustan

The Consuming Passions of
Iconic Women Performers of India

MADHUR GUPTA

RUPA

Published by
Rupa Publications India Pvt. Ltd 2023
7/16, Ansari Road, Daryaganj
New Delhi 110002

Sales centres:
Prayagraj Bengaluru Chennai
Hyderabad Jaipur Kathmandu
Kolkata Mumbai

Copyright © Madhur Gupta 2023

P-ISBN: 978-93-5702-103-6
E-ISBN: 978-93-5702-087-9

First impression 2023

10 9 8 7 6 5 4 3 2 1

The moral right of the author has been asserted.

Printed in India

I miss you mummy...

CONTENTS

CONTENTS

FOREWORD[1]

As entertainers and bearers of age-old traditions, we have to
often face the adversities thrust upon us by the continuous
cycle of this unrelenting time. Thus, I was quite happy to
read Madhur's book, *Courting Hindustan,* where he not only
features some exceptional women entertainers of India but
also grazes through the mystical lanes of fiction and facts to
bring out the outstanding lives lived by them.

Often referred to as courtesans, these women were not
just entertainers but also repositories of high art and culture.
They had a strength to their character that was rare in their
times and my family has personally been acquainted with two
of the many women written about in this book.

Begum Hazrat Mahal's husband, the last Nawab of
Awadh, Wajid Ali Shah, was a disciple of and patron to my
great-grandfather Kalka Prasad and his brother Bindadin
Maharaj. Begum Hazrat Mahal, as my family history tells
me, was born in absolute poverty but was a brilliant artist.
And that is what made her rise through the ranks, so much
so that when the Nawab was exiled to Matia Burj, she took

---

[1]As translated from an audio recording in the Hindi language

the reigns of Awadh in her hands and acted as regent to her son who was appointed the new Nawab. I am from Lucknow myself and reading the episode in this book brought back several memories of my hometown.

Then, reading about Jaddan Bai made me reminiscent of my father Pandit Acchan Maharaj whose disciple she was. My amma used to tell me that Jaddan had an exceptional voice and was trained by great maestros like Moinuddin Khan Sahab among others. Her *thumris* and *bhav* were quite a delight to watch and then when she became a pioneering music director in the burgeoning Bombay (now Mumbai) film industry, it certainly opened several doors for other women from non-traditional backgrounds to enter the industry. Her daughter Nargis was also inculcated into being a beautiful actress. Having said that, I have heard from amma that even Jaddan Bai, in her times had to face a lot of hardships before she was able to make a mark.

Conquering hardships and making a mark in history seems to be a running theme in the life of these women entertainers and this is what *Courting Hindustan,* I believe, celebrates. The revealing historical analysis of looking at these women through the sociopolitical lens of their time adds another layer of intrigue to the reading.

Many blessings to Madhur for creating this piece of literary art at such a young age and congratulations to Rupa Publications for their constant pursuit of bringing out books on our rich performing arts heritage.

Late Pandit Birju Maharaj
Kathak guru, choreographer, music composer and singer

INTRODUCTION

The epic accounts of Lord Rama's (Vishnu's avatar) win over the demon king Ravana or the brave Arjuna in the battlefield of Kurukshetra are some of the first visuals that come to mind when thinking of epics like the Ramayana and the Mahabharata. Unfortunately, we find ourselves a little ignorant of the formidable names of Shikhandi or Shabari, who are only fleetingly mentioned in these colossal sagas even though they had crucial roles to play. Folklore, mythology and even history have always favoured male characters and the narratives we read are often not offering any scope to women who might have developed strong inroads by themselves if the focus wasn't always on idolizing hypermasculine characters.

If even women personas like Sita, Draupadi and Ahalya—who were considered the epitome of modesty—had to battle their way up in being remembered as women of courage for their sacrifices; then the efforts and endeavours to celebrate women who were considered devoid of any fabricated notions of *lajja* (as entertainers and public performers, have been even fewer and far between). But the ripples these public women—or courtesans, as we now call them—created in the still pond of history have often been far reaching. These brazenly independent and fierce women achieved incredible glory in their lives while keeping their art intact.

In antiquity, it was typical for the best looking women in the country to devote themselves to the gratification of not just one, but many individuals. These women competed to acquire the *Nagarvadhu* (town's consort) honour, and it was certainly not perceived as a stigma. Their quoted prices could surge to 100 *karshapanas* an evening, making their treasured gilts even greater than that of many monarchs.

As per the ancient religious guidelines relating to sanctuary and temple worship (*Agamas*), dance and music were compulsory elements of daily prayers to divine beings in temples. *Devadasis* (Dev=Divine, Dasi=Servant) and *maharis* (Maha=Great, Nari=Woman), between the sixth and thirteenth centuries, had a high rank and pride in local culture and were extraordinarily affluent, often seen as the guardians of music and dance. During this era, royal patrons provided them with donations of property, assets (both in terms of land and livestock) and ornaments.

Tawaifs became a predominantly north Indian enterprise, fundamental to the ethos of the Mughal dynasty from the sixteenth to nineteenth centuries. It is also well known that younger nawabs-to-be were sent to these women of culture to study *tameez* (good behaviour) as well as *tehzeeb* (etiquette). This included the opportunity to discern and enjoy great music, literature and poetry and even pursue it as a lifelong activity. By the early eighteenth century, courtesans were a core feature of the sophisticated society of northern India.

The protection and patronage of the Mughals in the Doab area and then the Nawabi cultural environment from the sixteenth century onwards made art-related professions a viable proposition. Several young women were educated in both forms of performance arts (Kathak and Hindustani classical music) and poetry (*ghazals* and thumris) to a great degree.

A tawaif's coming of age was marked by a festival called the *Missī* ritual, which involved the ceremonial darkening of her teeth and lips. Courtesans in the north would integrate dancing, singing (notably ghazals), reciting poetry (*shairi*) and entertaining their patrons in *mehfils*. Much like the Geisha culture of Japan, their primary aim was to offer quality entertainment to their visitors.

Throughout the Deccan as well, the tawaifs enjoyed a rather prestigious role in the Nizami culture and as they were considered musicians, it was customary for all the tawaifs to perform in wedding ceremonies. Usually after these weddings, a group picture was taken for memory. Interestingly, there was always a spot for the tawaif in these group pictures as they were a symbol of affluence, since, only the wealthy could afford their services. These courtesans were also an indispensable part of numerous other ceremonies and gatherings, such as, the *Bismillah* ritual, the *Urs* ceremony and so on.

In the south of India, there were devadasis and maharis who were dedicated to temples and were even married to the deity. Choosing an auspicious day, the temple priest would tie a cloth—taken from the deity himself—around a young girl's forehead. That, along with the tying of the marriage knot around the girl's neck, made her a *nitya sumangali* or one who would remain married until her death. These girls then became wives of the temple deity and were responsible for all duties—from waking him up, dancing for him while he ate, to singing and putting him to sleep. The temple dancers would also engage mortal beings as their partners. These partners could range from a temple priest to the monarch of the region. It wasn't considered indecent by the high society of those times for the women to take on suitors—it was an accepted norm.

These courtesans were a central character in the enunciation of the profound puritanical insecurities that formed the reality of Indian modernization. Created over the nineteenth and twentieth centuries by a complicated entrapment of customs with re-enforced cultural significance, it is not really unprecedented that the image of the courtesan continues to be of lasting interest across a wide variety of realms. These realms range from colonial (and even post-colonial) policy, economy and philosophy, to foundational patriotic discourse as well as mainstream pop culture. The invisibility of these courtesans in scholarly debate, with no enthusiasm as a topic for any significant scholarly research work is, however, not entirely unexpected, given how artists in most cases live on the fringes of society.

From the little research that has been done to archive the works of courtesans—as per Dr Moti Chandra in his book *The World of Courtesans*[1]—it can be seen that the terms used for

---

[1]Chandra, Moti, *The World of Courtesans,* Vikas Publishing House Pvt Ltd, 1973.

courtesans traditionally were *datta*, *mitra* as well as *sena*. In north India, notably in the Awadhi region, tawaifs typically kept 'jan' or 'bai' attached to the end of their names as a marker of their social standing. Besides this, the names also differed according to the region, such as devadasis of Tamil Nadu, maharis of Orissa, jogamma of Karnataka, muralis of Maharashtra, maibis of Manipur and so on.

These courtesans were artists who were carriers of the nation's enormous history, creating cultural movements by their strokes and the turnings of their wrists. These holders of enormous instincts should not be thought of just as the creations of a *kotha* or as commodities who performed to appease the monarch or to receive a heavy hand of gold. At the core of the institutional values of courtesans lay a deeper, divine purpose of uplifting the mundane world of mortals, allowing them to envision the bigger picture. The metaphysical was always a parallel stream which flowed alongside the institution of courtesans, even though it has been brought down by socio-economic upheavals in the last century.

These women were entities of great significance to their patrons, so much so that they were even exchanged as dowry valuables. Thanjavur devadasis, Gauri and Kanthimathi, were sent to Baroda as part of the dowry of the princess Chimnabai once she entered the royal household of the Maharaja of Baroda, Sir Sayajirao Gaekwad III, as his queen in 1885. This could be the first instance of a south Indian dance group landing in north India.

The worth of the temple dancers turned court dancers can be assessed by this following anecdote. Maharaja

Sayajirao founded a *Kalavant Khatha* (the Department of State for Artists), which recruited and supervised musicians, dancers, painters and others. Gauri and Kanthimathi were solely accountable for their dance group when it came to presentations and were each compensated a lavish ₹433 per month (comparatively, the *nattuvanar, mridangist* and *thuthikarar* together received a far lesser ₹282).[2]

Gauri and Kanthimathi danced and entertained the Maharaja two times a week once he had finished his meal. Sayajirao, who didn't actually understand any Tamil or Telugu, is believed to have said that he did not need to understand the words as the essence of the verses were there in the performance itself. The performers also orchestrated five new routines for the Maharaja, mainly in Hindi, employing Bharatanatyam *mudras* and *adavus* along with several other imaginative gestures as they rendered various scenarios from their repertoire.

From the term 'nach' (meaning dance), the terminology of *nautch* appeared. Starkly different from devadasis and maharis who used to perform ritual and religious dances in the Hindu temples of India, nautch was essentially a court art. Nautch, performed only by women, developed into many forms in early colonial India, three of which were quite significant and popular: the *mor nach* (a peacock dance that is said to attract peahens), *patang ka nach* (a dance imitating kites and kite fliers) and *qahar ka nach* (a palki pallbearer's romantic and provocative dance).

---

[2]Minai, Cassidy, 'The Devadasi Video Mystery Solved! Gujarat and Its Bharatanatyam Legacy', *Cinema Nritya*, https://tinyurl.com/2s3c92ys. Accessed on 13 January 2023.

Traditionally, the nautch group's musicians commonly played four instruments: sarangi, tabla, manjira and sometimes, dholak. A fifth instrument, a harmonium, was added only at the turn of the twentieth century. Singers stood while singing in courthouses, royal residences and the dwellings of wealthy benefactors. Amusingly, while performing in the residences of poorer patrons and appearing in public, they remained seated.

Pran Nevile, a renowned author and scholar, in his book *Nautch Girls of the Raj,* has said:

> From time immemorial Indian poets have sung praises of the 'public woman', the professional entertainer. The epics give us a colourful description of her intimate connection with royal splendour. The Puranas highlight her auspicious presence as a symbol of good luck. Buddhist literature also testifies to the high esteem in which she was held in society. She appears through the ages in different incarnations from apsara [celestial virgin] in divine form to ganika [attendant], devadasi [spiritual dancer], nartika [ordinary dancer], kanchani, tawaif [cultured professional courtesan] and nautch girl [dancer member of the professional troupe].[3]

The conquest of the region of Awadh by the British in 1856 may be regarded as the earliest execution warrant for the ancient enterprise of courtesans. Suddenly, the British, the new patrons, didn't really value the courtesan culture and these women were classified as carnal criminals. Cultural

---

[3]Nevile, Pran, *Nautch Girls of the Raj,* Penguin Books, 2009.

intellectuals rejected courtesan culture as social debauchery. Not another thought was given to how these pioneering women made a significant contribution to the continuity of traditional dance and musical styles.

Some British, although quite well settled in their idea of what was not acceptable, still had an understanding of this art:

> Jealousy and love are hardly ever better portrayed than by the dark flashing eyes, and unrestrained passion, of an Indian natch girl. Very few English admire this exhibition on the first representation, but by repetition it ceases to disgust, and at length, in many cases, comes to form the chief enjoyment of life. It is a fact, however, that whenever this fatal taste is acquired, the moral being of the man becomes more and more enervated, until its healthier European characteristics that are lost in the voluptuous indolence that enthrals the generality of the western Asiatics.[4]

The hypocritical character of the colonial masters came to light when on one hand, they detested even the sight of these 'temple harlots' yet on the other hand, they forced these women to prison cantonments against their will for the pleasure of their soldiers. The Cantonment Act of 1864 and its revised version Contagious Disease Acts were an attempt to not only slander and bring down the name of these professional women entertainers but also an attempt

---

[4]*The English in India and Other Sketches. By a Traveller*, Longman, Rees, Orme, Brown, Green, and Longman, London, 1835.

to degenerate an entire industry, reducing them to carnal slavery.

The British view of devadasis was one of deep-rooted misunderstandings stemming from misogyny. These women, who devoted themselves to their regional Hindu temples, had sustained intimate ties with men from a high socio-economic class. These ties were typically polyamorous romantic affairs with a number of social superiors.[5]

This violated the conventional British understanding of mortal union and spiritual behaviour. The erotic aspect of the devadasi professionals was mostly rejected by the British. The British government then concentrated on the sexual placement of the devadasis in Indian society and introduced laws accordingly. The British regarded the conventional religious Hindu practice of committing such young ladies to the shrine as slavery of a juvenile. From 1860s onwards, prosecutions for 'temple harlotry' became much more popular. The tensions between Indian and British society became increasingly evident as British lawmakers passed further legislations against devadasi traditions. Inevitably, the then IPC (Indian Penal Code) conferred various activities of devadasi culture as a legal crime.[6]

While British sensitivities became offended by the sexual conduct of devadasis, the new masters were bizarrely

---

[5]Levine, Philippa, 'A Multitude of Unchaste Women: Prostitution in the British Empire', *Journal of Women's History,* Johns Hopkins University Press, Vol. 15, No. 4, 2004, pp. 159–63.

[6]Kannabiran, Kalpana, 'Judiciary, Social Reform and Debate on "Religious Prostitution" in Colonial India', *Economic and Political Weekly,* Vol. 30, No. 43, 1995.

unfamiliar with the customary privileges enjoyed by them—which, for some reason was not even investigated. Within the Hindu legislation, devadasis were given land and ownership rights, otherwise unthinkable for women at that time. Ironically, while many forms of slavery beneficial to the British were tolerated, devadasis, which was starkly a religious agency, was identified as an illegal mode of prostitution.

The British officials, knowing their shortsightedness in banning devadasis, issued a variety of weak and appalling explanations for the prohibition of courtesan and devadasi culture. One reason given for was that this prohibition was critical for the protection against homosexuality in India.[7]

The power and authority these women performers commanded have been outlined in Veena Talwar Oldenburg's paper, *Lifestyle as Resistance: The Case of the Courtesans of Lucknow*. Her analysis of the civic tax office records from 1858–77 reveals that the tawaifs were in fact the largest and highest tax paying class, with 'the largest individual earnings of anyone within the city'.[8] The article also mentions the systemic repression done by the British on the courtesan establishments after the rebellion of 1857.

Oldenburg states:

The courtesans' names were also on lists of property: (houses, orchards, manufacturing and retail

---

[7]Levine, Philippa (ed.), *Gender and Empire*, Oxford University Press, 2007, pp. 134–55.

[8]Talwar Oldenburg, Veena, 'Lifestyle as Resistance: The Case of the Courtesans of Lucknow, India', *Feminist Studies*, Vol. 16, No. 2, 1990, pp. 259–87.

establishments for food and luxury items) confiscated by British officials for their proven involvement in the siege of Lucknow and the rebellion against British rule in 1857. These women, though patently non-combatants, were penalized for their instigation of and pecuniary assistance to the rebels. On yet another list, some twenty pages long, are recorded the spoils of war seized from one set of 'female apartments' in the palace and garden complex called the Qaisar Bagh, where some of the deposed ex-King Wajid Ali Shah's three hundred or more consorts resided when it was seized by the British. It is a remarkable list, eloquently evocative of a privileged existence: gold and silver ornaments studded with precious stones, embroidered cashmere wool and brocade shawls, bejeweled caps and shoes, silver-, gold, jade-, and amber-handled fly whisks, silver cutlery, jade goblets, plates, spittoons, huqqahs and silver utensils for serving and storing food and drink, and valuable furnishings.[9]

If a government wishes to bring a profound conversion in the mentality of an entire generation, it takes to influencing the root of all understanding—education. The same thing happened in British India as well. Equipped with a western degree, willing to prove their worth to their British masters, several Indian *babus* and *memsahibs* resolved to put an end to the once majestic courtesan culture in India.

British sensibilities, due to their limited understanding of Indian society clubbed all women entertainers—whether

---

[9]Ibid.

they practised high arts or were street performers—as women of low moral character. This led Indians with a misguided sense of morality to move for the banishment of these glorious performers completely. It can be safely inferred that because these unorthodox women did not serve any British cause, they became victims of censorship.

The Madras Devadasis (Prevention of Dedication) Act proved to be the final nail in the coffin against courtesan culture. This was sadly brought around by the very Indians who were supposed to revel in the rich performing arts heritage of our nation. In his attempt to 'save' the devadasis from a life of 'debauchery', Muthulakshmi Reddi introduced the bill in the Madras State Assembly in early 1930, but it was only passed under the leadership of O.P. Ramaswamy Reddiyar (popularly known as Omandur Reddy) in October 1947. Due to heavy objections by the devadasis across the Madras State, the recommended bill was adopted only as a private act and not as a public legislation.[10]

Several women from traditional performing arts communities lost their livelihood, home, dignity and honour due to the introduction of this act. But even during such unrestrained onslaught against their culture, these women performers remained steadfastly devoted to the pursuance of their lifelong dedication. There is a sad but evoking anecdote of Mylapore Gauri Ammal, the last standing devadasi of the ancient Kapaleeshwara temple of Madras (now Chennai). During the growing surge of anti-devadasi resentment, unrest

---

[10]'1947: Madras Devadasis (Prevention of Dedication) Act Passed', *Frontline*, 10 August 2022, https://tinyurl.com/mtbdeked. Accessed on 13 January 2023.

and the emergence of statutory stigmatization of the regime, Gauri was forcefully expelled from her residence at Kutchery Lane by the temple authorities. It is then reported that she chose another residence from where the gopuram of the temple could be seen via the window. She did her *gopuram darshan* performance at night from her apartment's window.[11]

The Madras Devadasi Act was just one of numerous decrees formulated in the colonial states and presidencies in British India (and later in independent India) that declared devadasis and other types of temple dancers unlawful. A few of these acts were, the 1934 Bombay Devadasi Protection Act, the 1957 Bombay Protection (Extension) Act and the 1988 Andhra Pradesh Devadasi (Prohibition of Dedication) Act. These acts sounded the death knell for courtesan and devadasi culture which was once the pride of the nation.

Oscillating between fact and myths, through *Courting Hindustan*, we relive 2,500 golden years of women who were elite traditional entertainers, musicians, singers, poets and dancers. This book also navigates how, over the centuries, courtesans withstood the sociopolitical and economic upheavals, subtly shaping society at large and becoming the repositories of art and high culture.

Courting Hindustan covers the lives of some of the most significant courtesans who went on to become empresses, queens, prima donnas, pioneering filmmakers, music directors, ace dancers and so much more. Many of them went on to rule kingdoms, some influenced religious movements

---

[11]Roebert, Donovan, 'Some Very Early Pictures of South Indian Dancers, Part 2: CA. 1695-1780', *Aspects of Pictorial Indian Dance History*, 31 July 2022, https://tinyurl.com/4nzvefeu. Accessed on 13 January 2023.

in their country and many were also awarded the highest accolades by the power institutions active during their time. However, even with these wins and accolades, they remained ostracized by the upper class.

The book navigates the chronological advance of the structure of courtesan culture. Tracing back to medieval India where Amrapali invited Buddha to have a meal with her, to mid-fourteenth to sixteenth century ladies who elevated themselves from the position of dancers to queens of kingdoms like Sardhana and Awadh. The book further features modern India's courtesans like the famed Bharatanatyam dancer, Balasaraswati, who was awarded the Padma Vibhushan by the Indian government. It also features Jaddan Bai who was one of the first film-makers of young India and Begum Akhtar whose singing prowess was appreciated even by the prime minister at that time.

The fabulous lives of these women remains largely undocumented and thus shrouded in a veil interwoven with facts and myths. Perhaps, this mystery is what further enhances the enchantment which envelopes their lives. This book has tried to explore the various categories of traditional performers like nagarvadhus, devadasis, maharis, tawaifs, nautch girls and so forth.

Selective documentation of history has frequently silenced the echoes of these powerful women. With that kind of negative paradigm shift towards courtesans, India's famous female performers have naturally been severely misunderstood. Yet, these women have survived the mar of time. This book is an ode to them, it is their unsung saga.

1

AMRAPALI

The Courtesan, the King and the Monk

...Black was my hair
—the color of bees—
& curled at the tips;
with age, it looked like coarse hemp.
The truth of the Truth-speaker's words
doesn't change.

Like a sheet of gold, well-burnished,
my body was splendid.
Now it's covered with very fine wrinkles.
The truth of the Truth-speaker's words
doesn't change.

Such was this physical heap,
now:
A house with its plaster all fallen off.

The truth of the Truth-speaker's words
doesn't change...[1]

What is this 'truth of the Truth-speaker'? Who is the 'Truth-speaker'? What were the speaker's words? Initially, the mind dwells on plenty such musings but then the cloud of mysticism clears and one focusses on the golden aura

[1]'Thig 13:1 Ambapali', *Dhammatalks.org*, https://tinyurl.com/2azvusk4. Accessed on 13 January 2023.

of this poetess who sojourns these mystical plains, talking of lost beauty, wealth and passions. Such is the story of Amrapali, a courtesan par excellence who once had kings and kingdoms at her feet but gave it all up to seek the ultimate truth.

In *Therigatha*, a Buddhist text—the ninth book of the *Khuddaka Nikaya*, consisting of 73 poems, 522 stanzas in all—early nuns (*bhikkhunis*) have recounted their struggles and accomplishments along the road to *arahantship* and spoken of the courtesan, Amrapali, with heartbreaking honesty and beauty. The book reveals the deeply human side of this extraordinary woman who was so enticing in her charms that she could be called the daughter of the tempting *Mara* who tried to seduce Prince Siddhartha (Gautama Buddha) with visions of beautiful women. This story serves as an inspiring reminder of our own potential to follow in the footsteps of enlightenment. Buddha's *Ambapalika Sutta,* too speaks of Ambapali—better known as Amrapali—who, at the pinnacle of her reign as a nagarvadhu, decided to give up her luxurious life and follow the Buddha.

ॐ

Amrapali wasn't always the captivating goddess of beauty, the superlative dancer or the exalted courtesan of Vesali that she went on to become. Born to unknown parentage around 600–500 BCE, she was found by a gardener at the foot of a mango tree. Thus etymologically, the name Amrapali—*amra* being the Prakrit and Sanskrit term for mango and *pali* stemming from the word *pallawa* and corresponding to sprouting of tender leaves—came to be.

Amrapali's hometown, Vesali (or Vaishali) was located in present-day Bihar and was the capital city of the Vajjian Confederacy or Vrijji Mahajanapada. A prime example of one of the first republics around the globe, Vesali was also the cradle for the warrior clan of Licchavis—with whom Amrapali competed, in her later days, to gain the attention of Buddha.

Although Amrapali's early childhood remains clouded in mystery, some oral retellings mention that she was brought up by a *natyachar* and his dancer wife. Her adoptive father never wanted her to learn dance, let alone present a full-fledged concert. Several folktales insinuate that the child prodigy learnt and mastered her art by sheer osmosis of what her parents practised and taught to other *ganikas*. Amrapali grew up to be a charming, talented and graceful maiden, gaining mastery over the *Chatushashti Kalas*, the 64 kinds of arts described in detail in the *Kamasutra* by Rishi Vatsyayana. It is believed that her beauty swelled with such intensity as she reached adolescence that a feudal lord by the name of Mahanaman, enchanted to no end by the young Amrapali, abandoned his kingdom and moved to Ambara village, a small hamlet in Vesali to be close to her.

Her acumen was not just restricted to her talents. Exceptionally ahead of her times in feminist sensibilities, with a fierce outlook towards life, Amrapali could be one of the first women's rights activist, as she negated gender inequalities and stigmas in many ways. One cannot help but agree that living the life of a pioneer is a wearisome path to tread, especially with the demanding task of breaking regressive social norms, trudging a clearer path for the future generations.

Amrapali was also a victim of her own talents. A young girl, full of dreams for her future, the adolescent was deeply in love with Pushpkumar, her childhood beau, wishing to marry him soon. But she had no inkling of the storm that was about to ravage her peaceful life.

~

Away from the realm of Amrapali's existence, high-level political movements were unfolding at the centre of Vrijji Mahajanapada. Manudev elected by an electoral college consisting of princes and nobles from the Kshatriya clans, including the Licchavis, was coronated as king. He was known for his insatiable carnal desires and was constantly on the lookout for young and petite damsels.

As per the *Jatak Kathas*, Manudev once caught a fleeting glimpse of Amrapali at a dance recital. He was so overpowered by the desire to possess her that he ordered the assassination of Pushpkumar on the day of their wedding.

According to *Therigatha* (verses 206–7), Amrapali in her last birth was supposedly born in the time of *Sikhī Buddha* and had entered the Order of the Buddha. The same verses also elaborate on how she accompanied the other bhikkhunis on a pilgrimage to pay tribute to a shrine, despite the fact that she was a novice. It was during this cortège that an arahant Theri spit in the stupa's courtyard. Amrapali, on seeing the dribbling, called the person who did this a 'harlot', not knowing who had made the blunder. It is said that she had to experience such tragedies in this reincarnation as a result of this comment.

Many young princes and noblemen vied to have

Amrapali's hand, sometimes the conflicts even led to mortal feuds. King Manudev, advancing his malicious plot to possess her, ordained in an official declaration in the Court of Elders that Amrapali be declared a nagarvadhu to avoid these growing hostilities among the noble gentry. Ever the champion of women liberation, Amrapali fought tooth and nail to break free of this regressive custom which deprived young women of the right to have a family, only to be forced into the murky realm of erotic pleasures. It must be noted that it was unheard of in the ancient Indian society for anyone, let alone a woman, to oppose the canons of political and religious establishments.

Amrapali's opposition caused colossal panic in the male-dominated Court of Elders and the ancient society of Vesali at large. The hue and cry of a woman refuting the decision taken by the head of state and the council portrayed them as weak. The issue escalated to an anarchic level and threatened the very existence of political stability in the state.

Shattered by the death of Pushpkumar and enraged that she was unable to save her love, Amrapali reluctantly consented with the court's decision to maintain the harmony of her people and to avert any further massacre on her account. But the reservoir of melancholic bitterness and hatred that Amrapali now amassed in her broken heart would rupture against the Licchavis (ruled by its sovereign, Manudev), in the future and would bring forth much shame for this brutal clan.

Amrapali had accepted the council's decision under the condition that they fulfilled her five demands: she would be provided with a house in the best locality; only one patron would be allowed inside her premises at a time; her fee would be 50 karshapanas; if there were a general search for an enemy or a culprit her house would be inspected only by the seventh day; and no watch would be kept on persons entering and leaving her house. The council accepted her terms and thus Amrapali was anointed as the mistress of Vesali.

As the *rajanartiki* of Vesali, Amrapali entertained several nobles. She was no ordinary woman of pleasure. Mistress of almost the entire kingdom, she had the right to choose her lovers, but could not be committed to any one man. Bestowed with several titles—including that of *Janpad Kalyani*, given to the most beautiful and talented girl of the kingdom for a period of seven years—Amrapali's price was high and her treasury grew much larger than that of some kings.

Her bedchamber, it is said, was known as *swapna kakshikha*, or the chamber of dreams, and it truly was so for many men who wanted to satiate their erotic desires. For Amrapali, however, it was equivalent to a golden cage. She was like a lotus in a muddy pond, her physical being was surrounded by uncultivated desires but her spiritual self remained untouched from any impurities. Along with being one of the most gorgeous women in Vesali and a dancer par excellence, her magnanimity and interventions towards uplifting the socially downtrodden were undisputed and carried on even as she reigned the courts of the monarchs.

Unlucky in love, Amrapali had to submit to the desires of a patriarchal society where she was treated no more than an extremely valuable object of luxury. However, soon the flickering flame of her amorous desires was reignited when Bimbisara entered her life.

∽

King Bimbisara, also addressed as Seniya or Shrenika in several Jain texts, was the king of Magadha. He lived from 543–491 BCE and belonged to the Haryanka dynasty. Known for his cultural achievements, Bimbisara was a great friend and protector of the Buddha.[2] According to Hiuen Tsang (the famous Chinese Buddhist monk, scholar, traveller and translator), Bimbisara built the city of Rajgir (Rajagriha), famous in Buddhist writings. A culturally evolved being, Bimbisara was an excellent musician and valued the importance of art and culture. He showcased a much culturally advanced society of ancient India.

Bimbisara's reign finds mention in *Mahavagga*, which also narrates the hostility between Magadha and the republic of Vesali. Bimbisara, who was a keen administrator, wanted to learn the intricacies of governing a democratic establishment like Vesali.

In oral historical traditions, one can find two accounts of how Bimbisara and Amrapali found themselves in each other's presence. The first retelling of this mythical legend states that the tales of Amrapali's beauty and talent soon reached far and wide, across the *mahajanapadas*. Bimbisara was enamoured by these stories and wished to see her. He attacked Vesali and then took refuge in Amrapali's residence itself. As a musician par excellence he would often sing to her. In due course, the two fell deeply in love with each other. It was but a few weeks later that Amrapali got to learn of

---

[2]'Bimbisara: King of Magadha', *Britannica.com*, 4 February 2009, https://tinyurl.com/28hhc9dv. Accessed on 13 January 2023.

Bimbisara's true identity. Angered, she asked him to call off the war and leave immediately. Totally smitten by Amrapali, Bimbisara readily agreed to her wishes. He did not care that it made him seem like a coward in the eyes of the residents of Vesali. In the coming months, Amrapali bore Bimbisara a son, who she named Vimala Kondanna.[3]

The second retelling of the meeting between the king and the courtesan in oral mythology mentions that on hearing about the beauty and charms of Amrapali, Bimbisara sought to get a courtesan of such calibre for his own city of Rajgir. Bimbisara, in disguise, entered the limits of Vesali and approached Amrapali's residence as a patron. The succeeding plot remains largely similar to the first retelling, where the courtesan was deeply impressed by the disguised king's musical talents and having fallen in love with him, bore him a son. This son later, joined the Buddhist Sangha and attained arhantship. When Bimbisara revealed his true identity to Amrapali, feeling cheated by the monarch of an enemy state, she asked the imposter to leave her city immediately. A broken Bimbisara returned to Magadha but gave due public recognition to his son and his significant other. In retrospect, this recognition caused backlash for Amrapali as the people of Vesali were not too happy about this relationship.

According to *Mahāvaṃsa*, an epic poem written in the Pali language around fifth century CE, Ajatashatru, son of King Bimbisara forcefully took over the kingdom of Magadha from his father and imprisoned him. Both

---

[3]It is said that it was a sermon preached by Vimala later in life that helped Amrapali develop insight and gain arahantship as per *Therigatha*, verse 207.

Jain and Buddhist traditions offer a slight variation on the details of Bimbisara's decline and ultimate demise. According to the Jain tradition, once Ajatashatru asked his mother, Queen Chellana, whether she had ever seen a father as loving and caring as Bimbisara. In response to this, his mother narrated the story of Bimbisara looking after young Ajatashatru when he had fallen sick as a newborn. Moved by this tale, Ajatashatru then grabbed up a hatchet and rushed to the dungeon to release his father by smashing all the iron shackles himself. However, when Bimbisara noticed him entering with a hatchet in his grasp, he mistook Ajatashatru for an assassin and decided that it would be better if he ended his life with his own hands. At once, Bimbisara removed the talaputa poison from his ring, closed his eyes and chanted '*Kevli pannato Dhammam saranam pavajyami* (I seek refuge in the dharma taught by the kevlins or omniscient),' and swallowed the poison, thus ending his life.

Buddhist scriptures differ slightly from this account, saying that Ajatashatru wanted to starve King Bimbisara to death. The Queen kept averting the inevitable by secretly carrying packets of food for the imprisoned king. Ajatashatru forbade the queen from contacting the former ruler after she was caught. Bimbisara's health deteriorated, but he found solace in gazing at the mountaintop where Buddha and his followers stayed. Ajatashatru then ordered that the windows in his cell be covered so that King Bimbisara could never again find peace in gazing at that mountain.

One fated day, when Buddha had come to town, Bimbisara is said to have seen Gautam Buddha and his followers through the cracks in his door. He found peace and ended up living just because he saw Buddha as well as his followers. When Ajatashatru learned of this incident, he ordered the soles of Bimbisara's feet to be skinned.

King Bimbisara couldn't even move after such severe bodily torment, so he sat in bed, growing weaker. Once Ajatashatru realized the monarch was still alive, he hired a barber to puncture the king's thighs with a dagger and pour salt, fire (made from khaira wood) and boiling oil on top of the cut. According to Buddhist scriptures, the great monarch's life ended in this vicious patricide.

On hearing the news of Bimbisara's demise, Amrapali was absolutely crushed. But cruel fate was not done tormenting this heavenly courtesan. It is believed that soon, Ajatashatru, the murderer of her paramour, was about to sneak into her life as yet another patron. The irony was such that Amrapali did not have a clue that this man was the son and assassin of Bimbisara.

∽

Digha Nikaya (a revered Buddhist scripture) has *Samaññaphala Sutta* as the second discourse which reveals the story of King Ajatashatru. He is said to have followed policies of conquest and expansion. The story goes that he invaded Vesali and it so happened that when he was injured during a battle, he was treated by Amrapali and that he then fell in love with the courtesan. But when the people of Vesali became aware of the affair, they had Amrapali imprisoned.

On realizing who Ajatashatru was, a dejected Amrapali gladly accepted the imprisonment as a way to punish herself for foolishly falling in love with the killer of Bimbisara. Ajatashatru was so infatuated with her that in the process of securing her freedom, he ravaged the city of Vesali. Furiously angered by the havoc that Ajatashatru caused to her people, Amrapali rebuked and rejected the barbarous king.

From a sociopolitical viewpoint, it is truly remarkable that during the ancient and classical era, women in the Indian subcontinent had a say in choosing or rejecting their partners—a trend that faced a steep decline as the historical periods advanced.

A series of emotional blows had gouged Amrapali's soul inside out. Deeply troubled by her tumultuous personal tragedies, she was like a fish out of water. Disillusioned by the fickle nature of mundane living, she was yearning for the higher truth of life and that is when Gautam Buddha arrived in her life.

∽

The *Mahaparinibbana Sutta* brilliantly chronicles Gautam Buddha's final trip into Paranirvana. This scripture also contains a very engaging story—Buddha's meeting with the courtesan Amrapali.

Gautam Buddha spent almost 40 years wandering over the gangetic plains of the Indian subcontinent with his congregation of *bhikkhus* after attaining enlightenment underneath the Bodhi tree. His excursions are chronicled in a slew of suttas that aren't in any particular chronological sequence until one reaches the commencement of the *Mahaparinibbana Sutta*.

The encounter of Amrapali and Buddha happens in

the second section of this sutta—when Buddha journeys to Vesali—and is one of the few suttas before Buddha's terminal sickness and subsequent events. Amrapali is believed to have found her way to Buddha as soon as she learnt he had arrived in Vesali and even asked him and the bhikkhus to join her for lunch the following day.

When the Licchavis learned that Gautam Buddha had come, they prepared a great number of fine carriages and drove out to meet him. This is when the battle between Licchavis and Amrapali for Buddha's attention begins. It ends with the Licchavis finally realizing in despair that Amrapali beat them, when Buddha reveals to them that the lunch had already been committed to Amrapali. A woman taking on a Kshatriya clan, is unheard of even in the contemporary scenario. This episode put forth this celestial courtesan in categories of those whom the world should never forget.

Buddha equates the Licchavis to 'thirty-three gods', who are presented as follows by the legendary Master Yajnavalkya: 'eight Vasus, eleven Rudras, twelve Adityas, constitute one and thirty; Indra and Prajapati, create three and thirty.'[4]

Ahead of their lunch with Amrapali, Buddha warns the bhikkhus to remain aware, lest they lose their minds over her.

Amrapali herself attended on the community of bhikkhus headed by the Buddha and served them with choice food, both hard and soft. The hard and soft food represents the

---

[4]Shah, Bipin, 'Ambapali of Vaishali, Buddha of Kapilvastu and Kings of their Time', *ResearchGate*, December 2020, https://tinyurl.com/h9vz9547. Accessed on 13 January 2023.

apple from the Garden of Eden (signifying the knowledge of both good and evil) which, when consumed, enlightens the partaker. The bhikkhus consumed the meal without losing their heads—that is, without becoming attached to or deluded by the experience). Amrapali then donated her grove called *Ambapali Vana* to Buddha and his Sangha, wherein he preached the famous *Ambapalika Sutta*.

Although the most famous, Amrapali was not the only courtesan who was moved by Buddha's preaching of the impermanent nature of life. *Therigatha* also mentions the courtesan, Addhkasi, who wrote a poem revealing how ageing had eroded every trace of her youthful beauty. The poem is an exquisite portrayal of the effects of ageing where only the truth does not change:

> All of the Kāsi countryside:
> My fee was equal to that.
> Having made that my price,
> the town set me as priceless in price.
> But then I became disenchanted with my body,
> and—disenchanted—dispassionate:
> 'May I not run again & again
> through birth & the wandering-on.'
> The three knowledges
> have been realized.
> The Buddha's bidding
> done.[5]

[5]'Thig 2:4 Addhkasi', *Dhammatalks.org*, https://tinyurl.com/brt8b7pc. Accessed on 13 January 2023.

Vimala, who was a former courtesan also found peace in Buddha's teachings:

> Intoxicated with my complexion
> figure, beauty, & fame;
> haughty with youth,
> I despised other women.
> Adorning this body
> embellished to delude foolish men,
> I stood at the door to the brothel:
> a hunter with snare laid out.
> I showed off my ornaments,
> and revealed many a private part.
> I worked my manifold magic,
> laughing out loud at the crowd.
> Today, wrapped in a double cloak,
> my head shaven,
> having wandered for alms,
> I sit at the foot of a tree
> and attain the state of no-thought.
> All ties—human & divine—have been cut.
> Having cast off all effluents,
> cooled am I, unbound.[6]

The narrative of Amrapali is essential to understand society's current attitude regarding courtesans. Despite her reputation as a gifted artist, she was chastised by the aristocratic princes

---

[6]'Thig 5:2 Vimalā, the Former Courtesan', *Dhammamtalks.org*, https://tinyurl.com/mryca4a5. Accessed on 9 March 2023.

of Vesali, who referred to her as a ganika.

Unlike the princes, Buddha, had no bias towards Amrapali. He dined at her home and acknowledged her grove as a donation to the Buddhist Sangha. This incident is sometimes cited as proof of his fair behaviour towards women. Nonetheless, with the progression of time and the compilation of the *Therigatha*, such prejudices against women of art seeped into the Buddhist fold as well.

The stories of Amrapali's passionate and conjugal relationship with Bimbisara have survived mostly through oral tradition and haven't even made it into the Pali canon of Buddhism. This may be because Bimbisara was a major royal supporter of Buddhism and his ties with Amrapali, a courtesan, may have tainted his reputation. Her canonical mention also concentrates only on the last years of her life, when she turned to Buddhism.

Nonetheless, Amrapali's early life and association with Bimbisara are mentioned in various chronicles of Chinese travellers who journeyed to India in pursuit of Buddhist texts. Amrapali's association with Bimbisara may also be referenced in the Buddhist Tripitaka's original Chinese manuscript. Whatever little information exists of the story of Bimbisara and Amrapali is from the Mahayana tradition, which did not have the requirement of portraying Bimbisara in a favourable light.

The *Gilgit Manuscripts* are a collection of texts from Kashmir's Gilgit area that allude to Amrapali's narrative in great detail. These are the Mulasarvastivada school of Buddhism's Tibetan–Sanskrit texts, which refreshingly consider her in high respect. However, the negative connotation of being a courtesan is still present in several portions of this text as well.

This negative cultural memory, since time immemorial, highlights a complex pattern, varying across time and place. But the irony is that Amrapali who was treated with hypocrisy during her lifetime has remained enshrined in the hearts and minds of mankind for centuries. During her lifetime she defied all existing norms; contested for equal women rights in an era when women were treated like no more than child bearers; and also stayed true to her art and admirers, getting the title of *Janpad Kalayani*. Amrapali will always remain the epitome of the perfect combination of art and beauty.

2

VASANTASENA

The Golden Courtesan

The clouds hang drooping to the mountain peaks,
Like a maiden's heart, that distant lover seeks:
The peacocks startle, when the thunder booms,
And fan the heaven with all their jewelled plumes.[1]

In ancient classical Indian civilization, the role of a courtesan was a problematic phenomenon of liminality. Such *varanaris* were free of marital bonds, they were no one's property and their abilities were intended for the public's enjoyment. In this way, their liminal status served as a rite of passage into the greater role of communal service. Their profession, of course, had the risk of putting them in a defenceless position; where they ran the risk of exploitation and losing their 'modesty' at the hands of some unscrupulous people.

However, there have been iconic figures that were so well-trained in fine arts and performance, in knowledge of *kavya* and *shastras* that they were considered to be assets to particular cities and honoured by kings and nobility. Indian classical literature showcases courtesans as colourful characters with shades of both sins and saintliness. Forced to live outside the accepted boundaries of sophisticated

---

[1]'Lightning: An Abhisarika's Beacon to Her Paramour's Abode', *Karpuramanjari*, 23 September 2015, https://tinyurl.com/wjen53mz. Accessed on 9 March 2023.

society, these maidens possessed immense wealth and independence. Trudging at the fringes of this society, the courtesans of classical India enjoyed advantages (and at times disadvantages) of both worlds.

Vasantasena, a renowned courtesan from the city state of Ujjaiyini, gained such acclaim that she found herself projected as the female protagonist of the Sanskrit drama *Mrcchakatika* or *The Little Clay-Cart*, possibly from the fifth century CE. There is a fine line between history and mythical legends. While one is completely factual, the other is loosely based on reality. What remains, at the core, can possibly be called the truth. Vasantasena's story also treads on similar ground, interwoven with facts and myths, but staying true to the indisputable portrayal of courtesans during India's classical period (from 200 BCE–1200 CE).

The play is set in the ancient city of Ujjayini during the sovereignty of King Pālaka, near the end of the Pradyota dynasty that made up the first quarter of the fifth century BCE. As identified in the prelude of this 10-act Sanskrit drama by Shudraka[2] who is said to be a Kshatriya king and a devotee of Siva, who lived for 100 years. A *dvija-mukhyatama,* Shudraka was well versed in the Vedas and scriptures and was also a great warrior. There exists a popular view that *Mrcchakatika* has been derived from an earlier play, *Charudatta* by Bhasa[3] (who lived in the early centuries BCE), since the first four acts of the plays share close similarities. Shudraka, it is assumed, added the

---

[2] A celebrated playwright from ancient India

[3] He is the first recorded Sanskrit playwright, having been born in India in the third century CE.

chapters of the rebellion and Vasantasena's murder to the original story. Based on this timeline, Shudraka can be said to have lived between the times of Bhasa and Kalidasa.[4]

∽

Mrcchakatika is innovative in many respects, since it deals with various problems that were considered peculiar for Sanskrit tragedies, such as—a courtesan's nuptials to a poor Brahmin or a political revolt in the background that overthrows the Brahmin–Kshatriya dynasty. Instead of godlike men, epic champions and legendary noble kings as the *nayaka* and pious princesses or noble empresses as the *nayika*; Shudraka's play chooses a good-natured but poverty-stricken Brahmin as the nayaka and an intellectual, resourceful and impassioned courtesan as the nayika. Gambling, adultery, property concerns, bribery, terrorism and punitive justice are among the various issues addressed in the play.

This brings us to the start of the play where Vasantasena works as a courtesan. Vasantasena has wealth and influence in Shudraka's play. She owns a vast mansion and has a firm grip over her staff and maids. She has earned her money by entertaining people with her elegance, singing and professional dancing. She is also said to have never offered her services to anyone herself. Her decision to pursue such a career while maintaining her honour and integrity is portrayed as impressive. Even before the action of the play commences on the day before the spring festival, Vasantasena

---

[4]A fourth–fifth century CE Sanskrit writer who is often regarded as ancient India's leading poet and dramatist

has just seen Charudatta, a poor but compassionate Brahmin boy, in the Kama shrine and has been charmed by him from afar. Departing from the norm in plays at that time, she does not wait for the nayaka to contact her like a *mugdha* nayika. Instead, she begins to plan a meeting with Charudatta. This opportunity arises at a critical juncture.

Through some illicit relation, Samsthanaka, the king's brother-in-law, is after Vasantasena. He addresses her with choicest derogations like 'o dancing whore', 'perverter of families', 'denosed harlot'; and remarks, 'You are a courtesan, think of yourself as a vine on the roadside, available to be plucked by any passer-by and smell.'[5]

Samsthanaka, escorted by his followers, Vita and Ceta, chases Vasantasena in a night of heavy rains. Vasantasena, carrying a chest of her jewellery, desperate to protect her honour, enters into the residence of Charudatta and using her presence of mind puts out the light with a wave of her flowing garments. Her intelligence and presence of mind shine through this dramatic sequence in the play.

When the danger is over, Vasantasena disclosed herself to Charudatta who treats her with honour and addresses her as 'Arya Vasantasena'. Vasantasena's curious mix of feminine qualities is highlighted in the way she balances her life as a public woman while remaining regal at the same time.

After seeking Charudatta's pardon for this inconvenient intrusion into his house, she requests him to keep her jewels in his custody. Vasantasena knows that the crooks are not

---

[5]'Two Famous Courtesans: Vasantasena and Miss Tu', *Journal of South Asian Literature*, Michigan State University, Vol. 12, No. 3/4, 1977, pp. 31–6.

only after her youth, but also after her wealth. Her faith in Charudatta, at least at this point, is not a matter of blind love. She decides to entrust her treasures to an honest man, from a practical perspective. Vasantasena is a woman of the world—she knows what to do, when and whom to trust and whom to avoid. Her sense of nobility, combined with her practical intelligence, have given her a position of novelty and exceptionality.

Even when it comes to pursuing the love interest with Charudutta, it is Vasantasena who takes the initiative. It is her handmaid, Madanika, who identifies in Vasantasena various signs of one falling in love and pesters her to reveal the name of the man responsible for her state.

Most of the nayikas in Sanskrit literature are dedicated to their lovers or husbands in a form of worship. In most plays of that time love is a recurrent theme, but it is generally through the inventiveness of the nayaka, that the nayika's expression of love comes to the viewer's notice. Bhasa's Vasavadatta, Kalidasa's Shakuntala, Bhavabhuti's Sita–these iconic nayikas express their love in a way that is almost inseparable from worship. Even Kalidasa's depiction of Urvashi, in his *Vikramorvasiyam*, is rather mellowed and idealized—very different from the disengaged, independent and self-sufficient Vedic Urvasi or the Urvasi in the Mahabharata—a bold, candid and forward woman full of desire.

Shudraka's Vasantasena selects her own path, distinguishing between love and worship. The play shows her as a skilled courtesan who understands the intricacies of her trade. In most Sanskrit plays, the nayikas converse with their *sakhis* (intimate friends and companions; also servants) about their love interests, how to dress themselves, and the beauty of nature, among other things. In this aspect, Vasantasena is unusually novel: she engages only in professional conversations with her servants.

When Madanika asks Vasantasena if the civility at a courtesan's house is always false, she responds by saying that as courtesans they come in contact with so many types of people, so they tend to pick up a fake civility. Vasantasena understands the difference between professional civility and sincere affection. The impoverished Brahmin Charudatta's compassion and scrupulousness is what captivates her first. The jewels she left with Charudatta were stolen and Charudatta, in keeping with his noble character, sent forward his wife's necklace to compensate Vasantasena for her loss, apologizing for his failure to keep her gems secure. Vasantasena is enamoured by his virtues and resolves to marry him.

The disappearance and subsequent restoration of the jewellery (later in the play) represents a significant turning point in the tale. Sarvilaka, a good guy who becomes a criminal due to lack of funds, steals the gems from Charudatta's mansion, oblivious to the fact that they belong to Vasantasena. He also has the desire to marry Vasantasena's maid, Madanika.

With the stolen jewels, he goes to buy the freedom of his beloved. Madanika recognizes the jewels and asks him to return them to her mistress. Overhearing this conversation, Vasantasena releases Madanika so that she becomes free to marry Sarvilaka. In this instance, Vasantasena behaves like a benevolent figure of authority. Praising her maid's honesty, she calls Madanika a 'free woman', which is indicative of how much importance she sets upon the freedom and dignity, especially of a woman.

Earlier in the play, she prepares herself for a rendezvous with Charudatta. She sends him a message and goes to meet him like a bold, *abhisarika nayika*—at night, through thunder and rains.

∾

Vasantasena's courageous nature speaks volumes about her character. At one point in the play, when Samsthanaka tries to get hold of her for a second time, she escapes, kicking him off. When he finally catches hold of her and is about to strangle the nagarvadhu in a solitary grove, she uses her presence of mind and gathers all her faith and courage to overcome her instinct to scream for help, as it would bring shame on her character.

Samsthanaka is not bothered whether Vasantasena is akin to a wayside flower or a respectable lady and is only befuddled at the impudence of this woman to reject his advances. In an era when obedience and subservience, either as a wife or as a courtesan, was expected of women, facing such strong disregard enrages Samsthanaka to no end, pushing him to crush this elusive flower. Even in his last moments of insanity he pleads to Vasantasena:

> I hurl myself at thy feet, O Great Eyed One.
> My hands, Ten toed, Clean-toothed One, are folded.
> Whatever wrong I have done in love's lunacy,
> Forgive me, nobly limbed one, I am thy slave.[6]

---

[6]Ibid.

To this Vasantasena calls out, 'Go away, your tongue is foul!' When Samsthanaka asks her if she thinks men are made of wood, she snaps back, 'Who can doubt it now?' Thus, at this final insult the lust enraged villain charges at the 'ornament of the city'.[7]

The events mentioned above occur when Vasantasena is leaving to meet Charudatta in a park outside the city for an outing. It is mentioned in the play that she sits in a beautifully carved carriage but soon realizes that she is in a gharry belonging to Samsthanaka, who is madly jealous of the love and favour she shows to Charudatta.

When his henchmen refuses to murder Vasantasena, Samsthanaka sends his retinue away and proceeds to strangle her and hide her body beneath a pile of leaves. Still reeking of rage and seeking vengeance, he expeditiously accuses Charudatta of the crime. Although Charudatta proclaims his innocence, his very presence in the park along with his son's possession of Vasantasena's jewels (this was before Sarvilaka came forward as the thief) implicates the poverty-stricken Brahmin and he gets condemned to death by King Palaka.

The corpse labelled as Vasantasena, however, turns out to be that of another lady. Vasantasena has already been rescued and brought back to life by a Buddhist monk who nurtures her in a nearby town. Just as Charudatta is about to be executed, Vasantasena enters and witnessing the enraged mob, intervenes just in time to save him and his wife from being burned alive on the sacred fire.

Arriving at the courts, the nagarvadhu retells the story

---

[7]Ibid.

of her near death and, following her brazen testimony, Samsthanaka is arrested. Following these events, the just Aryaka deposes the wicked King Palaka. His very first gesture as the newly declared sovereign is to restore Charudatta's fortune by giving him an important position at court. In the final act, following this pleasant change of fortune, Charudatta exhibits his enduring virtue and charity by appealing to the King for pardon on behalf of Samsthanaka who is subsequently declared free.

ᔔ

Though Vasantasena enjoys becoming a 'wife' at the end, that title does not belittle her strong individuality. In truth, she is not a 'selected' bride—she picks her man, rescues him from dishonour and death and then marries him. This union only required the consent of a 'transformed' society led by a new monarch who had emerged from the ranks of the people. The play unmistakably portrays Vasantasena as a strong lady who yearns for a family and motherhood.

Earlier in the play, after spending the evening with Charudatta, she wakes up to discover his kid, Rohasena, crying because he does not have a golden toy-cart like his wealthier neighbour's boy. Vasantasena steps forth and fills Charudatta's son's small clay cart with all of her golden trinkets, basking in the warmth of motherly devotion. As a result, the free-willing sex worker becomes a motherly figure. Though not submissive and passive, she is nonetheless faithful and fervent in her love. By the end of the play, her desire for motherhood was accepted and appreciated even by Charudatta's first wife, Dhuta.

Her resolute love and motherly feelings place her as a

woman of power in the institution of ideal womanhood, as traditionally depicted in other Sanskrit play-texts. A woman branded as 'impure' by profession, Vasantasena in many respects proves herself to be more respectable than many who are quick to judge and criticize her. Though not much factual information is available about her, through the medium of the play, we can see her as an independent, candid, strong-willed, persistent and intelligent woman.

3

ROOPMATI

The Melodic Mistress

When love is lost, do not bow your head in sadness; instead keep your head up high and gaze into heaven for that is where your broken heart has been sent to heal.

Leaving ancient India enveloped in its classical romanticism, we now move toward medieval India whose dalliances take a further dramatic colour.

Rani Roopmati—who rose from the ranks of a singing girl to becoming the queen consort, only to be abandoned later and meet a tragic death—is a classic example of how beauty can be a curse as well. Such was the splendour of this maiden, that her name literally means—the bearer of unbound beauty.

Roopmati and Baz Bahadur's tale is one of love found and lost, now blurred by the passages of time. This immortal love story was first chronicled in poetry by Ahmed-ul-Umari in 1599 during the latter half of Emperor Akbar's sovereign reign, exactly 38 years after the fatal day when Baz fled, leaving Roopmati unprotected.

After being passed on from one hand to another over years, finally this poem reached C.E. Luard. It is then that the forgotten love saga was translated to English in 1926 by L.M. Crump, under the title, *The Lady of the Lotus: Rupmati, Queen of Mandu: A Strange Tale of Faithfulness*. The book also included 26 poems presumably written by Roopmati herself.

To give the readers an idea of Roopmati's beauty, here's an excerpt in Ahmed-ul-Umari's words:

> And of the dividing line of her hair what shall be written? It was as the river Ganges in the land of Hind. Strange outshone the parting of the hair of her head, even as a flash of lightning that cleaveth the midmost hour of night. The parting of her hair was a ray of sunlight or a strand from the rosary of Sulaiman or the dividing of night in twain.[1]

∽

Sixteenth century in India was a sort of cultural renaissance. Performing arts was evolving like never before, and the Malwa region—covering the present day Indian states of Madhya Pradesh and south-eastern Rajasthan—with its rich cultural heritage was proving to be the fountainhead of these artistic developments.

Before being mesmerized by the love story of Baz Bahadur and Roopmati entrenched in mellifluous music and poetry, one must take into account their contemporary political scenario to comprehend their lives and times. It is worth remembering that the Afghan–Turkish tensions tainted the early Mughal reign in northern India. The Lodhis had been defeated and driven out by Babur. Later, the Afghans commanded by Sher Shah Suri deposed Babur's son, Emperor Humayun, from the crown. Later, when Akbar was establishing his power, he dispatched expeditions to the

---

[1] Mahmood, Parvez, 'Lady of the Lotus', *The Friday Times*, 30 March 2018, https://tinyurl.com/5ap8ey7k. Accessed on 13 January 2023.

mainland to fight the Afghan lords who were friendly with the Suri empire. Baz Bahadur from Malwa, some 700 miles south of Delhi, ruled in a territory where the current states of Madhya Pradesh, Gujarat, Rajasthan, as well as Maharashtra converge.

Shujaat Khan, Baz Bahadur's father, the administrator of Malwa under Sher Shah Suri, died in 1555, the year in which Humayun returned from exile and reclaimed his kingdom from the Suri dynasty. Baz Bahadur later obtained his realm and chose to declare independence from Mughal rule. Numerous Afghan militants who came to India as staunchly orthodox assassins lost their militaristic edges and surrendered to the attractions of the Indian plains, becoming supporters of art, music and the finer things in this world.

Unlike his predecessors, Baz Bahadur was an accomplished poet and musician, indulging his passions even as a ruler. During one such musical *baithak* Baz Bahadur came across Roopmati. Legend goes that Abu'l-Fazl ibn Mubarak (also called Abul Fazal), the grand vizier of the Mughal Emperor Akbar, once said that Roopmati was renowned world over for her beauty, singing and poetic prowess.

The exact location of Roopmati's residence differs across various sources. As per popular Malwa lore, Roopmati is said to be the daughter of the local chief of Dharampuri, which may approximately be located in the Dhar district of central India near river Narmada. In the book, *A Memoir of Central India Vol. I*,[2] Sir John Malcolm writes that Roopmati

---

[2]Malcolm, John, *A Memoir of Central India Vol. I*, Thacker, Spink and Co., 1880.

was a dancing girl, residing near present day Sarangpur. But local accounts differ and another version traces Roopmati's descent from a small hamlet called Tandarpuri, which is near today's Maheshwar, again on the banks of river Narmada.

The sacred river Narmada revered by the Malwis of central India, seems to play a key role in Roopmati's legendary life. According to folk tales of the Malwa region, this beautiful maiden was the daughter of river Narmada and thus, shared an inseparable affinity to the river. It is believed that as a boon from Narmada, the chief of Dharampuri was blessed with a daughter. This birth story can be traced to a folktale according to which, the chief found Roopmati in a basket while taking a dip in the holy river.

Further advancing the plot of Roopmati's mystical birth, several medieval texts that treat the river Narmada as a Goddess say that Narmada revealed to the chief of Dharampuri in a dream that the girl was her daughter. Narmada is also said to have revealed that Roopmati will be a celebrated artist and a queen, reigning over vast dominions, both physical and metaphysical, with her unrivalled beauty, intellect and vocal prowess.

∽

Young Baz Bahadur was not a keen statesman and spent most of his time, wealth and resources in the pursuit of the arts. Once, when this young prince of Malwa was on one of his hunting expeditions and separated from his retinue, the lost prince overheard a mellifluous tune from a nearby grove. The sovereign, who had a discerning musical ear, could not help but follow the source of this enchanting melody. Soon, Baz found himself in a hidden spot where he stumbled across a petite Hindu maiden humming the beautiful tunes with deer, birds and even the trees swaying to the melody of her voice. He inquired about her name and then commenced a thorough discussion about musical treatises, ragas, melodies and so forth with her. Deeply impressed by the conversational skills of this golden beauty, Baz was eager to win her hand and heart.

To make her his, Baz respectfully proposed marriage to Roopmati, which she kindly but firmly declined. On being further coaxed by the lovestruck king, Roopmati replied, 'When the Rewa [the local name of Narmada] shall flow through Mandu, I will be your bride, but not till then.'[3] Roopmati knew that the feat she demanded was impossible, as Mandu lay on a raised plateau and the river flowed downhill and could never change its natural course and flow up, till the king's palace. But Baz Bahadur was adamant to make Roopmati his queen.

He assembled the engineering strength of his state and with an axe in hand went ahead to forge a canal from Narmada leading all the way to Mandu. Acknowledging the magnitude of his unrelenting love, the Goddess Narmada appeared in Baz Bahadur's dream and commanded, 'Desist from thy rash attempt, but receive the well-merited reward of thy love; repair to Mandoo, to a spot which overlooks our flood; search there for our sacred tamarisk, and dig wherever it is found; beneath it thou shalt come to a pure spring, which, being tributary to

---

[3]'Historical Romance: Rupmati and Baz Bahadur', *Notes on Indian History*, 22 January 2015, https://tinyurl.com/mr2nxym6. Accessed on 13 January 2023.

us, is part of our divinity. Thither bear thy bride, to live, as she has often sworn to live, on the borders of her natal river!'[4]

Thus, Baz went on this conquest of find the tamarisk, dug the natural spring, and constructed the now famous Rewa Kund. The king also built a palace near it and constructed an underground aqueduct leading all the way to the *hammam* of the palace so his beloved would not have to leave the comforts of her chambers to bathe in the holy waters of this spring.

To this day, it is a popular belief that it was only due to Roopmati that the river Narmada chose to spring up at a spot in form of the Rewa Kund (which otherwise is known for its dry and arid climate). Thus, came into existence, the famed Roopmati Pavilion, perched majestically on the edge of a 365-metre-high cliff overlooking the Nimar Valley to the south of the Baz Bahadur Palace.[5] Having fulfilled his love's wishes, Baz Bahadur again went to Roopmati to ask her to accompany him to Mandu and marry him in a grand ceremony.

However, the chief of Dharampuri, Roopmati's adoptive father was not too happy with this alliance. Unwilling to give his special daughter away to a Muslim prince, the Chief thought it was better to poison his daughter instead. Just as the innocent damsel was about to gulp down the bowl of fatal concoction, Baz came up with his army, engaging the Chief and his small troop in a skirmish and carrying off Roopmati to Mandu, finally making her his queen.

---

[4]'History of Mandu: The Ancient Capital of Malwa', *Archive.org*, https://tinyurl.com/2p8ubyx4. Accessed on 13 January 2023.

[5]'Afghan Architecture in Sandstone', *The Hindu*, 11 May 2018, https://tinyurl.com/4bd9e5tu. Accessed on 13 January 2023.

In a somewhat more mundane version of Roopmati's story, as linked by Ahmed-ul-Umri in his work, Roopmati is said to be the child of Jadu Rai, a Brahmin native of Sarangpur. Baz's father supposedly awarded him this village as a *jagir* (vassal state). Jadu Rai welcomed the monarch to a feast on his very first envoy to his estate. Baz Bahadur overheard Roopmati's song while in residence and then saw her in person. He was caught off guard by the girl's stunning beauty and was in awe of her ethereal singing. After taking command of the state upon his father's death, Baz requested Jadu Rai for Roopmati's hand in marriage in exchange for the fiefdom of Sarangpur. In 1555, she joined the harem, but because no wedding ceremony was held, she was regarded as a concubine rather than a legitimate wife in this retelling.

The beautiful palace built by Baz Bahadur was a one of a kind airy retreat for Roopmati. Here the lovebirds could enjoy the gentle breeze wafting in from the kund and the lovely scenery all around them. Roopmati could gaze at her natal stream Narmada from a hilltop nearby and pay her daily obeisance in peace.

It is widely believed that Roopmati used to have these *darshans* of the river goddess Narmada every morning as soon as she woke up. Then she would descend from her palace to take a bath in the Rewa Kund. Her life in this country residence was one of leisure and love.

From any version of the story, it is quite apparent how deeply Roopmati preferred the glories of nature to the grandeur and splendour of court life. There are several ruins of leisure palaces, like the Hindol Mahal, Baz Mahal, Rani

Roopmati's pavilion etc., which one can find even today in the surrounding areas. With Roopmati being immersed in the practise of music, Baz too let go of his inhibitions and they remained drenched in the pursuance of cultural activities, especially music.

Baz Bahadur was renowned as an expert in the Hindustani style of Indian classical music. Just like Tansen, he too had received education in music under Adil Shah Sur and later from the Gwalior *gharana* established by Raja Man Singh Tomar. It is a popular belief that since Baz Bahadur loved Raga Bhoop and Roopmati loved Raga Kalyan, they were amalgamated form the popular Raga Bhoop Kalyan.

Those were the days when Baz would address love poems to Roopmati and she would wittily reply to his poems with some of her own. These love poems are believed to be the major sources through which, even today, one can trace the oral history of Malwa region in the medieval period.[6] Baz Bahadur, a generous patron, is known to have kept a retinue of around 400 court musicians at Mandu who were experts in playing shehnai, sitar, tambur, veena and so forth.

He would often call upon gatherings of musicians for analytical discussions about Indian classical music, classifications of ragas and various gharanas, and so on. Roopmati was a proficient singer in the Dhrupad style of music and was also an able instrumentalist, delving into the veena, sitar and dilruba.

$\backsim$

---

[6]Ejaz, A.D. (ed.), *Rani Roopmati*, Ratan and Co. Book Sellers, Delhi.

Overindulgence of any habit is a curse. Baz Bahadur proved this saying by ignoring his responsibilities as a statesman. His unbound devotion to the pursuance of music, wine and his addiction to the fairer sex made him a weak commander of his legions, which, in turn, invited widespread unrest in his already small principality. The deterioration and slackness in his state administration instigated corruption and in turn dissatisfaction in the ranks. The state affairs of Mandu were being handled through external interference while its King was intoxicated in music and poetry.

Akbar was at the centre of power while Baz Bahadur was busy merrymaking with his consort. It was in 1561 that Akbar took advantage of the confusion in Malwa and sent his army to conquer the much-sought-after trade routes, which went through there.[7]

Besides political and strategic advantage, Akbar also had a personal equation to settle with Baz Bahadur. Familial enmity ran deep between the Suris and the Mughals. Humayun (Akbar's father) was ousted from India by the Suris who then took over the reins of his empire. Baz Bahadur, who was a direct descendant of the Suri clan, had publicly declined to become a vassal of the Mughals once Akbar ascended the throne. The public disobedience of Baz even after Akbar's orders mixed with a longstanding family feud and political unrest gave the Mughals the perfect opportunity to stake claim on Mandu.

Akbar, knowing Baz Bahadur's infatuation with

---

[7]'Baz Bahadur, Last Sultan of Malwa', *Notes on Indian History*, 19 July 2019, https://tinyurl.com/mr3m3y8t. Accessed on 13 January 2023.

Roopmati, is said to have cleverly written to him requesting him to let Roopmati visit the Mughal court so that even Akbar could hear the mellifluous voice of this enchantress. When Akbar received an extremely ill-judged reply from Baz Bahadur stating how the Mughals should send over their women to Mandu to entertain as well, Akbar's wrath knew no bounds and he ordered the commander-in-chief of the Mughal army to attack Malwa.

Adham Khan, the son of Akbar's much respected wet nurse Maham Anga, held the position of the commander-in-chief at that time. He, along with Pir Muhammad as second-in-command, arrived till Sarangpur with the intimidating Mughal army without facing any opposition. The Mughals knew how important this conquest was, as the trade routes into Gujarat, Gondwana, Deccan and even Rajputana could be controlled if they laid siege on Malwa.

Daunted by the imperial Mughal forces, the wine-drenched Baz Bahadur wasted no time in leaving his treasures and the entire harem, including Roopmati, at the mercy of Akbar's army. He headed south-west, across the rivers Narmada and Tapti, to Khandesh.

As the erstwhile ruler was disposed off and chased away to Khandesh, the generals of the victorious army were free to unleash unspoken atrocities and cruelties on the leaderless masses of Malwa. Houses were looted, men burnt alive and women and children raped indiscriminately. These horrors left a blot on the reputation of Akbar as a just and wise ruler.

Blinded by her love for Baz Bahadur even after his cowardly behaviour, Roopmati lamented thus on hearing of her beloved's abdication:

Tan main jeora rahat hai mangat hai sukh raj.
Roopmati dukhya bhai bina Bahadur Baz.[8]

(There is an intense burning in her body
She wants her Sukh Raj [Baz]
Roopmati has gone destitute in pain
Without the brave Baz.)

∽

There are a couple of retellings of how this unfortunate courtesan met her end when her lover left her at the mercy of the barbarians.

One version of the folklore states that when Baz Bahadur was preparing for war, he had ordered the caretaker of the *zenana* (women quarters) to put everyone to the sword, even his beloved Roopmati, in case his defeat was certain. It was considered a better destiny for the women to die rather than be captive slaves of the invaders. On receiving the news of Mandu's army being vanquished and the enemies approaching the fort, the caretakers got down to their brutal assignment and murdered several innocent girls of the harem. A ruthless guard was appointed especially for Roopmati, on whom he inflicted several brutal cuts, before leaving her for dead.

The other and more popular retelling of Roopmati's demise mentions how Adham Khan hastened his approach towards the fort of Mandu once Baz Bahadur retreated into the jungles, defeated. His men were able to seize the entire women's quarters and were also able to capture Roopmati

---

[8]Tiwari, Chandra Kant, 'Rupmati: "The Melody Queen of Malwa"', *Proceedings of the Indian History Congress*, Vol. 38, 1977, pp. 244–9.

before she committed *jauhar*. The lusting invader wanted to take this melodic beauty.[9]

At Adham Khan's insistence Roopmati agreed to meet him. Dressed in the finest of jewels and glittering draperies, this abandoned consort of Baz Bahadur sat in the carriage making its way to Adham Khan's canopy. She had a veil drawn over her face and the attendants thought she was asleep when her head tilted freely. When an eager Adham Khan lifted Roopmati's veil, all he found was a lifeless corpse. Roopmati, shattered by the cowardly desertion of Baz Bahadur and unwilling to submit to a barbarian, had swallowed the fatally poisonous, powdered diamonds and left this world forever, humming an eternal tune of love.

Another version of the story is based on the manuscript by Ahmed-ul-Umri which reads: '...and he [Adham Khan] asked Roopmati herself to transfer her love to the conqueror of her country. That virtuous lady advised him, openly saying that it was not the warlord's glory to attempt to humiliate the name and lameness of the shattered Afghans, for heaven may rain down that exact humiliation on the conqueror's shoulders on the day of retribution.' [10]

Adham Khan was so drunk with victory that he lost all reason and discernment. Roopmati exhibited neither

---

[9]Jauhar, sometimes spelled Jowhar or Juhar, was a Hindu practice from the Indian subcontinent of mass self-immolation by women. This was done to avoid capture, enslavement and rape by an invading army when facing certain defeat during a war.

[10]'Historical Romance: Rupmati and Baz Bahadur', *Notes on Indian History*, 22 January 2015, https://tinyurl.com/mr2nxym6. Accessed on 13 January 2023.

humility nor surrender when she heard this speech. Instead, she became even more adamant in her determination not to give up her life if a way out could be found. She asserted her intentions and escaped the capital on the next day itself. She is said to have disguised herself as a flower seller.

After three days, Adham Khan visited the harem, full of love, only to discover that Roopmati had fled. He had a difficult task ahead of him. He dispatched 15 of his best cavalry to apprehend her. By then, Roopmati had made her way over the intervening land, despite a thousand impediments, and was only 20 miles from Sarangpur when Adham Khan's chase squad caught up with her.

The squad had discovered that a lady had sought safety in a hamlet and had summoned her brothers to come and rescue her. Roopmati's brothers arrived and battled, but were killed. She was captured once again and forcefully taken back to Mandu.

Ahmed-ul-Umari, in his manuscript, says that Adham Khan believed that with time her sadness would wash away. The same manuscript then goes on to describe how even after Roopmati's repeated pleading and attempts to explain herself, the victorious commander, consumed by desire, refused to give up. Roopmati said:

> O Adham Khan, thou sayest that beauty and elegance are mine, but of what use would these be to thee? They'll crumble to dust if I'm around. My brothers are no longer alive, and I have no desire for the life of a day. The imperial throne from which we derived our content has fallen to the ground, and all of my brothers have died in order to maintain my miserable

existence. I beg that a lesson may be learned from thy noble heart, and that thou mayest leave us unhappy creatures in peace.[11]

'Although that four corners of the Earth join to rob me of connection with thee, I would make sacrifice of all my worldly joy, all my dreams of Paradise, and all that within is, for one minute of thy love,' Adham Khan responded.[12] Roopmati requested for three days to let her grief subside after this response practically eliminated any hope for her freedom. When Adham Khan arrived in the bedroom on the designated day, he discovered Roopmati dead, having poisoned herself.

∽

While Roopmati was suffering, where was Baz Bahadur? It's reasonable to say that when she bravely chose to die as a last resort, Baz was the coward who fled to Khandesh, where he was later ambushed by Akbar once again. In this occasion, Akbar was beaten and Baz reclaimed Mandu, only to surrender it again in 1562 to Akbar. He escaped once more, but in 1570 he finally submitted to Akbar. He lived under the reign of Akbar, the same emperor whose army, headed by Adham Khan, was responsible for the death of Roopmati.

Till date, there is a mausoleum in Ujjain that was built in the shape of a tank, in which this queen of music was laid to rest. Baz, who was not so *bahadur* (brave) after all, did however request to be buried near Roopmati. The melodic

---

[11]Ibid.
[12]Ibid.

mistress now lies silent in the graveyard of history where she still pines for her lost love and hums Raga Bhoop Kalyan in memory of all that could have been.

4

BEGUM SAMRU

The Dancing Girl of Sardhana

Among all who had opportunities of knowing her, she bore the character of a kind-hearted, benevolent, and good woman; and I have conversed with men capable of judging, who had known her [Begum Samru] for more than fifty years. She had uncommon sagacity and a masculine resolution; and the Europeans and natives who were most intimate with her have told me that though a woman and of small stature, her rudb (dignity, or power of commanding personal respect) was greater than that of almost any person they had ever seen.[1]

All of four feet and a half, Begum Samru had a will that could put the might of emperors to shame. Believed to be born to a nobleman in Kutana, a small town in Meerut district near Delhi, Begum Samru was brought up as a dancing girl in the red-light districts between Delhi and Agra. She is said to have risen to such heights of power that when she died, her total wealth was estimated to be around 55.5 million gold marks ($40 billion today).[2]

[1]Goswamy, B.N., 'The Begum of Sardhana', *The Tribune*, 8 December 2019, https://tinyurl.com/yckkr8mr. Accessed on 27 January 2023.
[2]Borpujari, Priyanka, 'India's Forgotten Power Broker—What Was Her Secret?', *National Geographic*, 5 July 2019, https://tinyurl.com/2exwwam4. Accessed on 27 January 2023.

One of the most emancipated women of her era, Begum Samru, who had once just been a young girl called Farzana, had adventure, turbulence and even treachery in her destiny. However, she rose above it all and became one of the wealthiest, most revered and awe-inspiring mother figures for many. The tale of this nautch girl turned mercenary turned queen began in the mid-1700s.

Although the facts of her origins are now obscure, different sources have called her Iranian, Arab and even Kashmiri. There is a letter written by Commander Bussy, a Frenchman, to Marshal de Castries, the royal minister of France, which states that she was of Kashmiri descent.[3] If this is believed to be true, it can explain her origins as a courtesan, since dancing had been a popular vocation in Kashmir from the olden times.

As per several verbal accounts, her father was one Latif Ali Khan, whose origins are also debated. Some say he was a fallen Mughal nobleman, while others believe that he was an Arab trader whose actual name was Asad Khan. This trader is believed to have taken in a Kashmiri concubine through whom he begot Begum Samru.

It is believed that her struggles began quite early in life when, after her father passed away, her stepbrother persecuted her and her mother and they were forced to run away to Chawri Bazaar or Bazar-e-Husn (which was then the famed red-light district of Shahjahanabad). After days of gruelling journey to Delhi, her mother, who had already

[3]Sharma, Mahindra Narain, *The Life and Times of Begam Samru of Sardhana [A.D. 1750–1836]*, Vibhu Prakashan, 1985.

been running a temperature, collapsed near a crowded *sarai* at Kashmiri Darwaza.

A tawaif from Chawri Bazaar, a Khanum Jan, who heard the child's cry, brought young Farzana to her kotha. Her mother, who was nursed back to health by the ladies of that brothel, found it natural that they had returned to their natural dwellings, from where it all began.

Khanum Jan's house was considered among the greatest in Chawri Bazaar for the entertainment of the elite. Khanum Jan enjoyed the patronage of men of all races and creed alike. Syed Hasan Shah, in his autographical work called *Nashtar* (published in 1790, translated into English by Qurratulain Hyder in 1992) has written these lines about Khanum Jan:

> She had a magnolia face and narcissus eyes.
> She must have ruined the piety of a thousand men.
> Our eyes met and I was struck by the arrow of love.[4]

Under this beauty, the dainty little Farzana began her training. She went on to become one of the most famous girls of Khanum Jan's kotha. Her beauty was truly aristocratic, and attracted many, including the mercenary, Walter Reinhardt. He coaxed her to elope with him and made her his begum. It was the perfect case of two peas in a pod—just like Farzana, Reinhardt too had a tempestuous past owing to his inherent opportunistic nature and his profession.

Eighteenth century India was a time of political unrest and European immigrants were known to take advantage of

---

[4]Raina, Kuldeep, 'Story of Begum Samru from a Nautch Girl to a Princess', *Kashmiri Pandit Network*, https://tinyurl.com/2h6sjcc9. Accessed on 27 January 2023.

the uncertainties to make their personal fortunes. One such immigrant was Reinhardt, who got the nickname 'Le Sombre' while he worked for the French East India Company due to his sombre facial features. Later, this nickname got corrupted to 'Samru' and that is how he came to be known across India.

According to some oral accounts, his origins were humble; his father is said to have been a stonemason in one of the poorest parts of Austria. To fight this drudgery and to seek his fortunes elsewhere, he is believed to have got into a French ship bound for Pondicherry, which he deserted as soon as it reached there. From there, he got himself enlisted in the exclusive army of the French East India Company. Even then, loyalty had not touched this man's soul, since he deserted them and joined the British East India Company for better compensation soon after.

As someone who could smell an opportunity from a mile away, he then went on to raise his own private army comprised mostly of other European mercenaries and shook hands with Mir Qasim, the Nawab of Bengal. He butchered numerous British citizens in India, which notoriously gave him the title of 'Butcher of Patna'.[5] With the fall of Mir Qasim at the hands of the British, Samru charged towards Delhi, and he and his army were ready to be hired by the highest bidder.

That bidder came to be the Mughal ruler Shah Alam II who also awarded him the principality of Sardhana (a small town in the Doab region), which later became his capital. At one point, he even became the governor of Agra under Shah Alam II.

---

[5]'Patna Massacre of 1763', *Azadi ka Amrit Mahotsav, Government of India, Ministry of Culture*, 1 November 2022, https://tinyurl.com/3mr5jaet. Accessed on 27 January 2023.

Samru was also employed by the king of Bharatpur; he had several soldiers from the Jat community in his army.

When Samru was in the 42nd year of his life and Farzana had just seen 14 springs, they met at Khanum Jan's kotha. Farzana, who was soon to become Begum Samru, had exceptional leadership qualities that, some might even argue, even eclipsed Samru's.

Thus began the journey of this nautch girl, who had the best of both worlds (Mughal and British) at her feet and had a string of lovers and suitors eating out of her hand as soon her husband died on 4 May 1778.

∽

Begum Samru and Reinhardt stayed together till his death, and the Begum even accompanied her adventurer husband on many sieges. It was, in fact, Reinhardt who supposedly taught Begum Samru all that he knew of politics, warfare and statesmanship.

When Reinhardt was alive, Jats were a predominant force in Agra. Najaf Khan, a major courtier of Shah Alam II, wanted to push them out of Agra, which had once been the prized possession of Mughals. So, he pleaded the newly crowned emperor Shah Alam II to get Reinhardt to switch sides and come over to the Mughal camp. This was in 1773 and Reinhardt's army had around 2,000 soldiers, a battery of artillery, including canons and war elephants, and European commanding officers, which made up a fierce force to reckon with. He was heavily bribed by the Mughals and thus, in the battle between Jats and the Mughals, Reinhardt and Begum Samru found themselves on the winning Mughal side.

As a compensation for his tactical support, Reinhardt got the sanad of Sardhana which yielded around ₹6,00,000 at the time. Suddenly a fortune monger had become a land magnate, but the British were still in hot pursuit of him. If it wasn't for the Begum's intelligent interventions, her husband would have been lost in the political power struggle between the British and the Mughals that had ensnared the Indian subcontinent at the time.

Begum Samru knew how to win the heart of the ruling class: she had to get drenched in their colour. Thus, after the death of her husband, it was at the behest of Reinhardt's troops—ranging over 5,000 men and 100 plus European generals from his private army—that Begum Samru was made the ruler of Sardhana.[6] There exist oral accounts of Reinhardt having other wives and children and even some accounts of his three children with Begum Samru, but they all lie under a thick veil of mystery.

Begum Samru, true to her shrewd politics, had her stepson, Zafaryab Khan declared unfit to rule under the pretext of him being a minor. The French were keen supporters of Zafaryab Khan but ended up backing the Begum. This was because both Reinhardt and Begum Samru received the patronage of Najaf Khan. Additionally, Begum Samru also had abundant wealth left to her by the innumerable campaigns that she and her husband had been a part of. This wealth solved not one but two problems—the private army of Sardhana could be paid for and the courtiers and soldiers

---

[6]Garodia Gupta, Archana, *The Women Who Ruled India: Leaders. Warriors. Icons.*, Hachette India, 2019.

saw Begum Samru as a respectable figure (who could lead completely into their forces in the future). This is how little Farzana bloomed truly and completely into Begum Samru. Her fate was sealed when the Mughal Emperor Shah Alam II declared her to be Walter Reinhardt's true successor.

Her story could have ended here and the widowed Begum could have led a lavish life full of her newly found riches. But Begum Samru's destiny was much bigger than just being a nautch girl or the widow of a rich husband. She ended up actively participating in politics and shaping the country's future while also introducing a new era of court etiquettes in her time.

∽

India of the late eighteenth century saw the intense power struggle between the British and the age-old Mughal empire. Begum Samru, at this time, quite intelligently introduced the age of multiculturalism in her court and applied it to herself as well.

Three years after her husband's passing, she converted to catholicism and built the largest cathedral in India at that time (Basilica of Our Lady of Graces) and even sent a portrait of the cathedral to the then Pope, Gregory XVI, in Rome. Even her court was filled with Europeans—French, Dutch, Belgians, Amish—but not many British. She threw lavish parties, mainly for the Europeans and she had a full-time band led by an Indian master to play at the balls.

Nevertheless, she was quite entrenched in her Islamic roots as well. She practised purdah, dressed herself in attires worn by Mughal women of the aristocracy, spoke Urdu and

Hindi, but not English. She would seldom be seen dancing at her own lavish balls. It was as if while wanting to appeal to the emerging rulers of new India, she also wanted to command equal respect among the old elites—the Mughals.

Begum Samru was also quite conscious of the charming effect she had on people. Deft in the art of conversing, she proved her mettle in political arbitration. Besides the verbal charm, she also had the grit and determination of leading an army into numerous battles. It won't be wrong to assume that the prowess and survival skills she had was owing to the early struggles she faced as a dancing girl.

∽

In 1783, Baghel Singh, the Sikh leader, had encamped just outside Delhi with 30,000 of his troops. This area, presently in Old Delhi, is known as Tis Hazari as a hat tip to these troops. Baghel Singh along with Jassa Singh Ahluwalia, sieged Delhi and laid claim on the Mughal throne. It was on Begum Samru's insistence and timely intervention that the Sikh leaders acceded to let the Mughal ruler come back to the throne (but only after their demands were met). The wise Begum Samru struck a deal on behalf of Mughals when Sikhs demanded the creation of five gurudwaras in Delhi. They also demanded that 13.5 per cent of the annual revenue of the leftover Mughal empire be paid to them as maintenance.[7]

It so happened that by the time Shah Alam II had acceded the Mughal throne, his empire was in such ruins that there came to be a saying, '*Sultanat-e-Shah Alam, Az Dilli ta*

---

[7]Ibid.

Palam', which meant that the empire of Shah Alam is only from Delhi to Palam (a suburb of Delhi). The Maratha chief, Mahadji Shinde, had taken over the regency of this puppet emperor and even when Sikhs signed a peace treaty with the Mughals, it was Shinde who signed that one-third of the annual revenue will be paid to the Sikhs on behalf of the emperor.

During this time, Zabita Khan, also known as Ghulam Qadir, became an ally of the Sikhs and even got Baghel Singh to convert him to Sikhism. He then changed his name to Dharam Singh, attacked Delhi in 1786 and held the puppet emperor at his mercy.

In his rage at not finding the hidden Mughal treasury (which was virtually non-existent by then), he had Shah Alam II blinded and committed many more gruesome atrocities against the Mughals. Khan is said to have dragged Shah Alam by his beard and scooped out his eyes with a knife. It is believed that he also made the Mughal princesses strip naked, which made them drown themselves in the Yamuna out of shame. Begum Samru rushed to help the blinded emperor on hearing the news.

The usurper tried to bribe Begum Samru but she outright rejected it due to a strong sense of loyalty towards her and her late husband's benefactor. Then, Khan changed his tactic and tried to hoodwink her by calling her his sister (to put her at ease) so that she would arrive at the Red Fort, where he planned to capture and kill her. Begum Samru took this in her stride and entered the Red Fort promising to help win the loyalties of the the remaining Mughal chiefs. She spent the entire day charming the crazed tyrant and as soon as night fell, her army took control of the entire fort and saved the terribly sick and injured Shah Alam. Khan was left at the mercy of Mahadji Shinde.

At times when she could not come to help herself, she sent her squadrons and artillery to help the Mughal emperor, for instance, to crush the rebellious Najaf Quli Khan. The Begum is said to have also ridden with the Emperor to many such campaigns into her late 70s.

Due to this gallantry and loyalty, Begum Samru grew even closer to the Mughal emperor, gaining the title of *'zebun nissa'* which loosely translates to 'ornament among all of women'. She was also given appellations like 'beloved daughter of the emperor', among many others. By the time Akbar Shah II ascended the throne after Shah Alam II, her influence in the capital had grown so much that he gifted her a park next to the Red Fort in Chandni Chowk, where she built her palace, now known as the Bhagirath Palace.

This palace was witness to several crucial moments in history, including the Revolt of 1857. James Baillie Fraser has spoken of Begum Samru, saying:

> It is a remarkable thing, and much to the credit of the Begum's troops, that some four or five of her battalions were the only part of Sindea's army that went off unbroken from the field of Assaye: they were charged by our cavalry towards the close of the day, but without effect; Colonel Maxwell, who commanded, being killed in the charge by a grape-shot.[8]

---

[8]Baillie Fraser, James, *Military Memoir of Lieut.-Col. James Skinner*, Cambridge University Press, 2012, p. 286.

∽

Begum Samru's appetite for adventure wasn't restricted to the battleground; she had a fierce love life as well. It is well recorded that after her husband's passing, she had a string of lovers. She had all the wealth, power and sex that a woman could ever dream of in those times. Yet, she yearned for love. She had become the ruler of a large land but in her heart, she was still the little Farzana who wanted a life of passion and romance like the one she had with Reinhardt.

Out of her many lovers, Le Vaisseau, a Frenchman certainly stands out. Vaisseau is said to have joined the ranks of Begum Samru's army in 1790. At that time, Begum Samru was a young widow of 28. Along with him, there was also this other suitor who comes up in oral retellings, often called George Thomas, who tried to woo her and proposed marriage quite a few times. Vaisseau was a jealous person, to say the least, and worked his charms on the Begum to poison her ear against his rival suitor. Initially, this trick did not work on the Begum who was well aware of how competing lovers work against each other, owing to her time as a courtesan. However, she fell for his charms as time progressed.

The Begum was highly refined in her upbringing with Khanum Jan and quite disliked the brutish, unkempt nature of George Thomas. Vaisseau, on the other hand, was unparalleled in charming the Begum. She was deeply in love with him and there came a point when she could do anything for him. Such was her fascination with this Frenchman that the Begum appointed him as one of the commanders of her army in only a few years since his joining. By 1793, they even secretly got married.

Her officers and even the peasantry of Sardhana were against Vaisseau. He was arrogant and treated anyone lower in the ranks with disdain. Additionally, he was also set on ruining George Thomas who was not only an able commander, but also a kind leader of the Sardhana principality and army. The Mughal Emperor, Akbar Shah II and her well-wishers tried to warn her about the error in choosing Vaisseau over Thomas but she refused to pay heed to their well meaning advice.

The news of her being with Vaisseau did not go down well with the forces and soon there was an outright revolt in the ranks. The commanding forces leading the mutiny marched towards Zafaryab Khan, to offer their allegiance to him and to uproot Samru from her seat of power. Meanwhile, a priest solemnized Begum Samru and Vaisseau's marriage.

Mad in love with the Frenchman, Samru decided to leave all her riches and power behind and retire with him. They decide to move to Chandernagore, near Patna, which was a French settlement at that time. Both the Begum and Vaisseau, like true lovers of lore, had made a pact that if anything were to happen to either one of them, the other would not live to see the sun another day.

As fate would have it, en route Chandernagore, which was supposed to be their new home, the couple were captured by Sardhana's forces. Some say that these forces were tipped off by George Thomas. The Begum, who was secretly carrying a dagger, stabbed herself. In the commotion when Vaisseau witnessed Begum Samru's lifeless body, he shot himself. But the Begum was still alive. She was brought back to Sardhana, treated back to health and held captive.

The British meanwhile were deciding whether to support Zafaryab or the Begum in this battle and finally decided to take Begum Samru's side. This decision was taken as Begum Samru still held much sway over the zamindars of the Doab region, and at that time, they needed all the military and financial support that they could gather.

The rebelling forces of Sardhana were not appeased by the Britisher's rejection of Zafaryab Khan and wanted the Begum off the scene too. At this time, there was another twist in this romantic tale when the Begum appealed to George Thomas to save her. Like a gallant beau, he did just as the Begum demanded. Thomas protected her and she was reinstated as the Begum of Sardhana.

There has been some critique about the Begum's treachery in signing a death pact with Vaisseau and then slyly bowing out of it later. These critiques, though partly right, are misplaced, as one must remember that before becoming a begum she was a courtesan and was not in the habit of fretting over a single lover. The hardships of her life did not give her the luxury to do so. She had to look out for her own survival. This is precisely what drove her to seek help from George Thomas as well.

This tumultuous period ended in 1793 with her being reinstated, but Begum Samru's struggles were not over yet.

ᔕ

At that time, being a powerful woman in India was no mean feat. There was not only a power struggle between various nationalities and sects but no one was also willing to share power with a woman.

By early nineteenth century, the British had expanded their imperialistic dreams and were on a power trip. They were annexing one state after another to quench their gluttonous ambitions. In 1803, Lord Wellesley asked Begum Samru to surrender her estate to the British without any conditions.

Begum Samru—who had struggled so much in her life to reach a place of power, respect and riches from the lowly lanes of Khanum Jan's kotha—knew how to manoeuvre this political situation expertly.

She sent her troops to help the Maratha leader Daulat Rao Scindia, Mahadji Shinde's successor, when the British attacked the Deccan (now known as the Anglo–Maratha wars). However, staying true to Reinhardt's tradition of being an astute judge of turning tides, she made her forces switch sides and help the British when their victory became imminent.

Although the British saw through this crafty war strategy, they didn't reject the Begum's support. They needed all the assistance to crush the Marathas and establish an empire. Nevertheless, the British remained wary of Begum Samru's overtures for years to come. It continued even after she played an instrumental role in freeing the British collector of Saharanpur from Sikh leaders.

She went on to openly support the British against the Marathas when Maharaja Ranjit Singh signed a treaty with the British. As a result of this, the British Governor General, Lord Cornwallis, let her keep the jagir of Sardhana without any annexation looming over her head. She was told to be cautious of any anti-British movements.

∽

Begum Samru saw quite a few upheavals in her lifetime but her grit, determination and astute mind kept her going from one thing to the other. Such independent women were unheard of in the late eighhteenth to early nineteenth century India.

Just like any other woman of power she too was feared by many, to the point of demonization. The prowess of the Begum grew so far and wide that she became a living legend in her own lifetime and several urban myths were associated with her.

James Skinner, an Anglo–Indian soldier, has been quoted saying: 'The people in the Dekhan [Deccan], who knew the Begum by reputation, believed her to be a witch, who destroyed her enemies by throwing her chadir [women's veil] at them.'[9]

Her palaces and religious institutions are still intact, even though she is long gone. Begum Samru continues to capture the fantasies and imaginations of drunken poets, moonstruck writers and lovelorn admirers of beauty till date.

[9]Goswamy, B.N., 'The Begum of Sardhana', *The Tribune,* 8 December 2019, https://tinyurl.com/yckkr8mr. Accessed on 27 January 2023.

5

BEGUM HAZRAT MAHAL

The Rebel Courtesan

> The Begum of Awadh shows greater strategic sense and
> courage than all her Generals put together...[1]

Renowned as North India's cultural capital, Lucknow is known as the city of the Nawabs, who are best remembered for their sophisticated, extravagant lifestyles and benefaction of the arts. Its districts were jam-packed with walled *baghs*, palaces, mosques, tombs and beautifully built mansions. The *zenana* or the ladies section of the nawab's household was symbolically known as the *pari khana* or the fairies' abode. The opulent central hall of the pari khana would be adorned with numerous chandeliers while a marble-floored patio, with porcelain flowerpots on the outside, set the stage for open-air events. It was linked to Lanka (an island in the middle of the canal) via a bridge in the Qaiser Bagh gardens. Life-sized marble statues and tall lamp posts lined the canal and provided a picturesque setting for the courtesans performances. The magnificent aesthetics of Lucknow were not limited to its architecture but also spilled into the performing arts.

Historically and culturally, Lucknow has had a tradition of courtesans. The pari khana also housed a large group of young, attractive and talented women—usually drawn from

---

[1]Dundoo, Sangeetha Devi, 'The Begum and the Mutiny', *The Hindu*, 17 January 2013, https://tinyurl.com/yfzyf6ee. Accessed on 11 January 2023.

the families of courtesans—committed to the promotion of music and dance. Kathak, one of the classical dances of India, originated in Lucknow. The courtesans in Lucknow, with their polished social etiquette and mannerisms, were a class apart. Many of them enjoyed unbound patronage of the aristocratic class and even the British when they were called upon to perform *mujra* or sing ghazals in special functions and private baithaks.

However, such hedonistic practises were banned during the reign of Amjad Ali Shah who—acting on the instructions of his Shia high priest, Sultan-ul-Ulema—ordered professional singers, dancers and musicians to leave Lucknow. But the *fatwa* seemed to have no sway over his son and heir apparent, Prince Wajid Ali, who continued to be a patron of the artists. Conversant with the art of playing the tabla and sitar, the Prince composed several musical compositions set to Hindustani ragas and indulged heavily in the arts.

Many great musicians and dance masters came to the pari khana to train the artists. The Kathak maestros, Thakur Prasad and Durga Prasad, were not only dancers in Wajid Ali's court but also teachers to those who lived in the pari khana.

The pari khana was heavily safeguarded by female sentries trained in martial arts and use of weapons. Wajid Ali had employed 192 female artists in the pari khana. If he desired an intimate relationship with any of them, he solemnized a *mutah,* which was later converted into a *nikah* if the lady was impregnated. Wajid Ali is said to have performed mutah with as many as 112 of these ladies.

౧

One female artist with whom Wajid Ali solemnized a mutah was Muhammadi Khanum, whom the world now knows as Begum Hazrat Mahal. She was born in Faizabad, Awadh, India. From being a lowly courtesan, she ended up being one of the acting wives of the last Tajdaar-e-Awadh. Her story is full of characters straight out of a novel—a poor girl who became a courtesan, a smitten Nawab who made the courtesan his mistress and then, the courtesan's transformation into an unrelenting queen who refused to give up her land.

Muhammadi's father, according to oral retellings, was Ghulam Hossein Ali Khan (commonly called Umber) and her mother was his concubine. Muhammadi was auctioned off by her parents and placed into the royal harem to continue in her mother's footsteps. She was taken into the zenana as a *khawasin* and was later promoted to a pari, eventually gaining the title of *Mahak Pari*. She only became a begum after being accepted as a royal consort of the King of Awadh, and the title 'Hazrat Mahal' was bestowed upon her after the birth of their only son, Birjis Qadr.

The protagonist of a twisted tale of fate, Hazrat Mahal's life was not untouched by controversies. It was a popular belief that courtesans indulged in liaisons with the rich and wealthy and often had more than one suitor, especially if they were renowned for their beauty and charm. It is believed that Mammu Khan, one of the generals of the Awadh army, was Birjis Qadr's actual father and not Wajid Ali Shah. Later, this belief got reaffirmed when Mammu Khan got appointed as the *deewan khanah* of the state after Birjis Qadr's coronation. He is also believed to have helped Hazrat Mahal in the execution of the British when they attacked Awadh in 1858.

Hazrat Mahal was born and raised as a courtesan and the sense of respect and deference that she wanted in her life was elusive. There is a famous story about how, once, when Hazrat Mahal had been performing at a royal soirée, some lewd comments made her put down her *ghungroos* in full view of the court and demand the king to give her a life of dignity. Even at the insistence of the king, she did not continue with her performance. Such was this feisty courtesan who later demonstrated the same courage in defending her home against foreign invasion.

∽

On the fateful day of 6 March 1858, British troops—English, Scottish, Sikh, Bengali and even Nepali—attacked Lucknow, which was then the jewel of the Indian subcontinent.[2]

The ruling nawab of the time had been preparing with pomp and gaiety for the ninth anniversary of his coronation as the tenth sovereign of Awadh. Unfortunately, this could never happen because the British, acting on their imperialistic desire for India, dethroned and banished the nawab just two days before the ceremony. However, the people of Awadh and their courtesan queen were not ready to give up their ancestral land without putting up a brave fight.

Awadh had been annexed around February 1856, along with many other such independent states. At that time, to whitewash their thievery and greed, the British manufactured several excuses. The reality, however, was apparent—

[2]Hegde, Vinayak, 'Warrior Begum of Awadh: The Untold Story of Hazrat Mahal's War on the British', *The Better India*, 17 August 2018, https://tinyurl.com/mv8xr2b9. Accessed on 27 January 2023.

Lord Dalhousie had a huge army and wished to control as much land as he could. By that time, Awadh's army was almost non-existent and Wajid Ali Shah, with timid docility, agreed to be pensioned off to Calcutta (now Kolkata). The Nawab soon left for Calcutta, arriving there in May 1856 with a huge entourage, many animals and cooks. He spent his remaining days in Calcutta, creating a mini-Lucknow in exile.

However, Begum Hazrat Mahal and her son were not part of the train of followers that left with the Nawab. A daring and enigmatic politician, the Begum still believed in fighting for the rights of her son and that of Awadh. She also had the support of many influential courtiers, aristocrats and the people of the state.

Bitterness was building among millions of common citizens and more gravely, among the thousands of sepoys who had enlisted with the British army to fight for them. Primed by the unashamed behaviour of the British, the fire was awaiting a spark. This spark was ignited in Meerut, where the sepoy, Mangal Pandey, refused to use the new cartridges issued for his rifle. The reason for this was the cow and pig fat used to grease the outer layer of the cartridges that the sepoys had to tear with their teeth before loading the bullets in their firearms. This assault on Hindu and Muslim religious sentiments (as cows are considered considered sacred for Hindus and pigs are considered impure for Muslims) was appalling to many. Though few rallied to his cause initially, after he was hanged, the rebellion swiftly spread from Meerut to Lucknow to even Delhi.

The revolt arrived at Awadh in the form of thousands of rebel sepoys. Begum Hazrat Mahal and her followers, including the local aristocrats of Awadh, had been comparatively hushed till then. But seizing the occasion, they quickly prepared themselves and overthrew the British authority in their state. This feat was achieved with the support of several local landowners, the nobility and even common peasants, who flocked under the Begum's banner. This revolt was a brilliantly timed move that stunned those who had thought the fighting spirit of Awadh was flickering.

Begum Hazrat Mahal's rebellion was ignited due to the nonchalant demolition of temples and mosques by the East India Company to make way for roads. Acting as a beacon of unity, she countered the British assault on religious freedom by retorting:

> To eat pigs and drink wine, to bite greased cartridges and to mix pig's fat with sweetmeats, to destroy Hindu and Musalman temples on the pretense of making roads, to build churches, to send clergymen into the streets to preach the Christian religion, to institute English schools, and pay people a monthly stipend for learning the English sciences, while the places of worship of Hindus and Mussalmans are to this day entirely neglected; with all this, how can people believe that religion will not be interfered with?[3]

On 5 June 1857, Begum Hazrat Mahal crowned her son Birjis Qadr, as the rightful Nawab of Awadh and Raja Jai Lal was appointed the military commander of the state. The battle of

[3]Sayed, Hares, *War, Violence, Terrorism, and Our Present World: A Timeline of Modern Politics*, Xilbris, 2017.

Chinhat, fought in a mango grove on 30 June 1857, brought matters to a head. The British were crushed and forced to withdraw to their fortified residency inside the city. Awadh was officially free of British rule from that day.

William Howard Russell, a reporter, sums up his opinion of the Begum at the time: 'This Begum exhibits great energy and ability. She has excited all Oudh to take up the interests of her son, and the chiefs have sworn to be faithful to him. [...] The Begum declares undying war against us.'[4]

Begum Hazrat Mahal assumed charge of affairs as her son's protector for the next 10 months. She enjoyed the backing of the nobles and the common people of Awadh and even the penultimate Mughal emperor, Bahadur Shah Zafar, accepted her rule.

Despite coming from a courtesan background and having no formal training in the art of state administration, she proved to be an able regent and a plethora of oral accounts (on both Indian and British sides) mention that this former courtesan was not shy to battle. Several accounts mention that she visited numerous camps to boost the morale of the soldiers with her blazing speeches and her able presence in various battles. It was under her guidance that the British were contained within the Lucknow Residency. These days of battle were later renowned in history as the 'Siege of Lucknow'.

The Begum was a valiant and sharp woman. She heroically fought the British with the assistance of Maulvi Ahmadullah Shah Nanasaheb Peshwa and several landowners. The battle

---

[4]Oldenburg, Veena Talwar (ed.), *Shaam-E-Awadh: Writings on Lucknow*, Penguin Books, 2007.

of Alambagh is mentioned in letters of gold in the annals of India's first war of independence. This is where the Begum, in a fit of contempt, put each and every British person present on the battlefield to death. Later, she announced throughout her state that in her dear land of Awadh, they shall not allow even a single British to remain alive.

She petitioned to the masses of Awadh to slay the British wherever and whenever they find them. The Begum favoured fighting the unjust British Raj staunchly rather than yielding to them and getting arrested. Staying true to the free spirit of courtesans, the Begum organized an army of women and appointed Uda Devi as its commander. Uda Devi played an active role in the 1857 insurrection against the Doctrine of Lapse[5], which required them to relinquish Lucknow. This story of Begum Hazrat Mahal was first reported in print in the 1971 Census reports by Pasi responders. Though no reference to Uda Devi was found at first, subsequent responders mentioned that a Pasi *paltan* liberated Begum Hazrat Mahal from British captivity during the battle of 1857.[6]

Many official British accounts of the battle of Musa Bagh in Lucknow stated that the Begum herself was present at the battles, combating and rallying around the rebelling masses that were fighting under her banner. She was sometimes even seen riding elephants to battles.

‿

---

[5]A policy of annexation of princely states initiated by Lord Dalhousie of the East India Company

[6]Gupta, Dipankar (ed.), *Caste in Question: Identity or Hierarchy?*, Sage Publications, 2004, p. 199.

While his fearless concubine, Begum Hazrat Mahal, chose to stay back and confront the British, Wajid Ali Shah was escorted out of Awadh by his spirited mother, Jenab Aliya Begum (famously known as Malika Kishwar). She had gone to London to inform Queen Victoria of the injustices the Company was unleashing on the people of Awadh (and India at large) but her pleas had fallen on deaf ears.

The British were quite adamant that it was their right to conquer lands in the name of 'modernizing' and 'educating' the indigenous masses. And so, a beaten and hopeless Malika Kishwar decided to return from London to India via France. She was hoping to convince the French to intervene.

But by this time, the exhausted Malika Kishwar's health was already declining rapidly and on 24 January 1858, she breathed her last in Paris. Her funeral was attended by representatives of Turkish emperors and a cenotaph was raised over her tomb. By the time the sad news reached the Begum, she had already begun to fight the British and crowned her son as the justified ruler of Awadh.

For the Begum, the news came as a dreadful shock, as the two had been been very fond of each other. The Begum focussed on fighting the British to do justice to Malika Kishwar's spirit.

∽

Begum Hazrat Mahal took care of the dealings of the state of Awadh regardless of her separation from Wajid Ali Khan. The British triumphed over many things that year—they captured immense stretches of lands and beautiful cities, looted wealth and built an empire. But even with the many gems of India that they stole, there was one they could never claim—Begum Hazrat Mahal. However, the concentrated strength of the British Army was too much to hold off for long and Begum Hazrat Mahal's rebel forces were ultimately defeated.

Many things worked against the total eradication of Company rule in India, especially in Awadh—the disunity among the rebels was one of the chief reasons. The British, on the other hand, had one commander-in-chief, with a single goal to crush each rebel force before moving to the next. They also had an unbroken supply line, technologically sound warfare and enormous amounts of money and resources.

Sadly, the British also had the assistance of many Indian kingdoms and even neighbouring countries like Nepal. The Begum only had her own will, disorganized allies and eventually, not enough firepower. Some spaces, like Sikandar Bagh, were crammed with the bodies of hundreds of massacred rebel sepoys.

Since the very beginning, the existing rebels and defenders; the leftover revolting sepoy regiments from all over North India; regular citizens of the city; and the soldiers and mercenaries from surrounding areas of Lucknow fought as they had never done before. Unfortunately, it all ended in a catastrophe.

Delhi and Kanpur had already been captured by the British army. Their soldiers were now marching towards Jhansi and Gwalior. In the midst of all this, a disorganized Lucknow could not hold out for long. By 21 March 1858, it was all over.

The British made several offers to the Begun—a hefty pension and a rule under them as their regent. But the Begum rejected them all. It was everything or nothing for her and that remained the case until the end. She outsmarted the British and slipped out of Lucknow before the war ended, making her way to the Terai regions of the Himalayan forests in the north. She fought fiercely at every step against the pursuing British regiments, before finally seeking sanctuary in Nepal.

'Why Nepal?', one may ask, especially when they supported the British in capturing many Indian kingdoms. Some accounts, in books such as Kumar Ghising's *Doon Ghati-Nalapani* and Amritlal Nagar's *Gadar ke Phool* propose that Begum Hazrat Mahal was of Nepali descent. Her Nepali ancestry, these accounts state, was one of the reasons why she opted for Kathmandu as her place of asylum.

While in banishment, she unrelentingly followed the developments in India and continually rebuffed offers to return. To one such proposal, she had quite famously responded: 'Do not tell me about such things, I am fully aware what you have done with the children of Tipu Sultan and with Bahadur Shah Zafar until your type of people will prevail, Lakshmi Bai and Hazrat Mahal will take birth in this country.'[7]

The British complained relentlessly, but the Nepali regime refused to hand her over. For over 16 years, the Begum resided in Kathmandu, gradually losing all her possessions. But she refused to come back and surrender.

Begum Hazrat Mahal is revered as one of India's bravest freedom fighters. The exiled Begum used to assist

[7]Bloks, Moniek, 'Begum Hazrat Mahal–The Rebel Princess', *History of Royal Women*, 20 May 2019, https://tinyurl.com/mtcw75b. Accessed on 9 March 2023.

the unfortunate even though she was going through hard times. She would part with her possessions without a second thought to help the deprived. Her fate barely seems like an adequate tribute to someone who could have led a life full of luxury had the circumstances been different. Her life is a lesson from the first war of independence in Indian history and is still relevant. The following couplet from Nawab Wajid Ali Shah best describes the courtesan who went on to become the famous rebel queen:

> *Gharo'n par tabahi padi saher mein, khude mere*
> *bazaar, Hazrat Mahal*
> *Tu hi baais e aisho araam hai garibo'n ki gamkhwaar,*
> *Hazrat Mahal*

> (Calamity fell on the houses in the morn; my bazaars
> were looted, Hazrat Mahal
> You alone are a source of comfort, O comforter of
> the poor, Hazrat Mahal)[8]

Begum Hazrat Mahal died in exile on 7 April 1879 in Nepal. She had assisted in building a mosque and had quite nostalgically named it 'Hindustani Masjid.'[9] It is said that when she passed away, she had no money, even for a grave. Her final resting place was in a tiny grave in a now encroached corner of the Jama Masjid in Kathmandu.

---

[8]Safvi, Rana, 'The Forgotten Women of 1857', *The Wire*, 19 November 2018, https://tinyurl.com/ye2xfvmb. Accessed on 27 January 2023.
[9]Alam, Md. Yousuf, 'Chronicle of the Forgotten Female Warriors: Begum Hazrat Mahal', *Tripura Times,* https://tinyurl.com/y5kcnfuk. Accessed on 27 January 2023.

It is noteworthy that there is no historical evidence to establish that the Begum was Nepali. This is just one instance of how bits of information about her Kathmandu link and many other significant details about her have not been substantiated.

Over 166 years later, it is challenging to sum up her leadership and inspiration. The freedom intrinsic to courtesan culture was also seen in the rule of Begum Hazrat Mahal—making her the famed rebel courtesan queen.

At that time, the Begum ruled the largest region of the rebel territory, commanded the most considerable rebel force of the battle and held out the longest against the British attacks. Such was the story of this courtesan queen who turned into a rebel and fought till her last breath for her people and country.

6

GAUHAR JAAN

The Gramophone Girl

Arey pathik giridhari su itni kahiyo ter
Brij jhar nayi radhika ab brij bhurat pher
Aaja sawariya tohe garva laga lu
Ras ke bhare tore nain... Sawariya...
Ras ke bhare tore nain...
Jehi chitawat tehi bas kari rakhat
Naahi padey man ka chain... Sawariya...
Naahi padey man ka chain...
Aaja sawariya tohe garva laga lu
Ras ke bhare tore nain...[1]

(O dark one, O beloved...
Your eyes are full of sweet syrup,
O beloved, your eyes are full of sweetness...
I agonize day and night, O beloved,
I agonize day and night for you...
I don't get peace unless I see you, O dear,
I don't get peace unless I see you...
O dark one, O beloved...
Your eyes are full of sweet syrup)

---

[1]'Gauhar Jan: Ras Ke Bhare Tore Nain...', *YouTube*, https://tinyurl.com/46br892z. Accessed on 9 March 2023.

This is the tale of a feisty woman who was way ahead of her time—the very first to use recording devices in India. It is the tale of a visionary who diligently and elegantly condensed a complicated musical style into two-and-a-half-minute recordings allowed by the discs. It is the story of a courtesan with all possible human frailties, exacerbated by a fortune made, then lost. This is the story of Gauhar Jaan, one of the biggest superstars who has all but vanished from public memory. Listening to Gauhar Jaan's first recordings, even now, intrigues one's imagination vividly. Her voice boldly rises over the hiss and clatter of the shellac disc displaying glimpses of her life and times. The end of some discs even contain her signature sign-off—'My name is Gauhar Jaan!'—in English, leaving one fascinated.

∽

Gauhar Jaan was born on 26 June 1873 in Azamgarh. She was raised as Ellen Angelina Yeoward and is widely known to be of Armenian ancestry. She was baptized in a Methodist Church at Azamgarh. Her father, William Robert Yeoward, used to work as an engineer in a dry ice mill. In 1872, he married Adeline Victoria Hemmings, Gauhar Jaan's mother, in Allahabad (now Prayagraj). Adeline, an Indian, was already skilled in music and dance.

Back in the day, when the British started landing in droves in the Indian subcontinent, their wives often preferred to stay back in England since travelling in those days was pretty adventurous. Thus, the concept of *biwi khana* came into being where the British officers married or took in Indian women as their wives or mistresses to run their households and look after the 'wifely duties'. Gauhar Jaan's mother was similarly taken in by William. The union between William and Adeline did not last very long. Gauhar Jaan's parents got divorced before she was six years old, after which she (along with her mother) migrated to Banaras (now Varanasi). As a result, Gauhar's inherent skills in dance, literature and music developed in the culturally bustling metropolis of Banaras.

Adeline turned to Islam and, in doing so, took the name of 'Badi Malka Jaan'. She was nicknamed Badi (older), since in those time three other Malka Jaans were widely known—Malka Jaan of Agra, Malka Jaan of Mulk Pukhraj and Malka Jaan of Chulbuli—and because she was the oldest of them, Badi Malka Jaan stuck to her. Later, even Gauhar received the nickname 'Gaura'.

Malka Jaan steadily became a famous courtesan, a renowned Kathak dancer and was celebrated for her dance and music skills. When her success and reputation continued to grow, they all relocated to Calcutta, where the financial prospects were considerable. Badi Malka Jaan established herself in the courts of the erstwhile Nawab of Awadh, Wajid Ali Shah, who had been exiled to Metiaburj, outside Calcutta. Within three years, Malka Jaan bought a property at 24 Chitpore Road (now Rabindra Sarani) for a princely sum of ₹40,000.[2]

While residing in this property, little Gauhar began her education, studying traditional Hindustani vocal music under the guidance of the two founding members of the Patiala

---

[2]'Gauhar Jaan', *Indpaedia.com*, https://tinyurl.com/5xbfbwjz. Accessed on 27 January 2023.

gharana—Mian Kallu and Ustad Ali Baksh Khan—along with learning kathak under the iconic Bindadin Maharaj. She then went on to learn *Dhrupad Dhamar* under Srijanbai, as well as Bengali *Kirtan* under Charan Das.

With such intense training, it is no wonder that soon Gauhar began writing as well as composing ghazals under the pen-name 'Hamdam' and then became an authority on Rabindra Sangeet[3]. Both mother and daughter were the manifestation of the secular tradition that Indian classical music is noted for. Although Gauhar was brought up as a Muslim, most of her writings and songs were about Krishna *bhakti* and many other tales from different religious backgrounds.

Gauhar had her *rang pravesham* at the court of the King of Darbhanga Raj in 1887. That was especially remarkable because she was just 14 at that time. Despite her tender age, the Maharaja was strongly pleased by her skill and appointed little Gauhar as a palace musician and dancer. Gauhar Jaan rose to become a master of *khayal, dhrupad* and thumri styles of singing. Her khayals were so exceptional that the great music revivalist, V.N. Bhatkhande, went on to proclaim her as the best female khayal singer in the entire Indian subcontinent.[4]

Her exceptional skills made her popular with the kings of the Maithili ruling family, who frequently welcomed her to their imperial courts. She was kindly called 'Gauhar Jaan Kalkattewaali' by her fans.

---

[3]Rabindra Sangeet, or Rabindro Songit, as pronounced in Bengali, is the soul of Bengal. Written by Rabindranath Tagore, the legendary literary personality, Rabindra Sangeet is a a collection of over 2,000 songs.

[4]'Gauhar Jan (1873-1930): The Diva', *Women On Record*, https://tinyurl.com/2pz29u39. Accessed on 27 January 2023.

ᘒ

At the turn of the twentieth century, the world was engulfed by rapidly changing technological inventions. The field of performing arts could not stay elusive for long. Emile Berliner invented the first commercial sound recording device in 1887 and branded it the gramophone.[5] Eventually, the mass manufacturing of music recordings was made possible using the gramophone and several discs that were made from each record. Soon after, in 1898, the Gramophone Company in London, England, was registered and produced hundreds of recordings each year.

In 1902, the pioneering sound engineer from America, Frederick William Gaisberg, was hired by the British Gramophone Company to start recording oriental performing artists. After a session or two with lesser-known musicians, he came across Gauhar Jaan who, by that time, had become the most celebrated female musician in Calcutta and even across the nation. She, in the truest sense, had become the reigning diva of her times.

Now, one must remember that when audio recording technologies came to India in the early twentieth century, it was the women who truly embraced and adopted this novel and unknown medium. Disregarding superstitious beliefs, circulated by male artists—that recording on evil English devices would infuriate the gods and make one lose their voice—they took initiative and recorded.

Not only did this help democratize music and carry it

---

[5]'Berliner's Gramophone', *National Museum of American History, Behring Center*, https://tinyurl.com/2p87t6br. Accessed on 27 January 2023.

out of the realms of the kothas and imperial courts, it also freed these female musicians from the clutches of exploitative patrons. It helped them break free from the restraints of being accessible only to the upper class Indian strata. Taking on Gauhar Jaan as a recording artist proved to be an expensive affair, since in those days her *nazrana* for a sitting ranged between ₹3,000–4,000[6] (an amount considered exceptionally high for the early twentieth century). Gaisberg graciously accepted this, given the heights of popularity that Gauhar Jaan enjoyed in those times.

But there remained a bigger and highly sensitive hurdle to cross—breaking all barriers of the Hindustani musical rendition. Since in Hindustani musical renditions, the *alaps* alone go on for several minutes and the proceeding raga rendition go on for hours—how would it be compactly fitted into a record in under three minutes? It was unheard of and quite unbelievable. Why couldn't the recording be longer than three minutes? Well, simply put, the technology did not exist at that time. The 78 rpm (revolutions per minute) shellac discs in those times could only record upto three minutes.

Both Gauhar Jaan and her recordist took on this challenge for which they received a lot of flak from the upper class public and music connoisseurs of that era. However, this move ultimately helped popularize Indian classical music among the public and democratized it. This style remained the norm until the emergence of LP recordings[7] several decades later.

---

[6]Jha, Tanya, 'Gauhar Jaan: The Forgotten Doyen of Hindustani Music | #Indianwomeninhistory', *Feminism in India*, 22 August 2018, https://tinyurl.com/yntr4u8b. Accessed on 27 January 2023.

[7]In 1948, Columbia Records introduced the long-playing (LP) record,

Gauhar Jaan chose a khayal in Raga Jogiya for the first-ever proper recording of an Indian performing artist and it bloomed in high octaves. To retain the essence of an hour-long khayal into a three-minute audio recording, she pioneered a peculiar way of delivering an expansive khayal in a short period of time. The resultant recording is vivid, and it also had an emotional touch, since the raga in itself evokes the feeling of detachment.

Her recording sessions commenced on 8 November 1902. As mentioned previously, her records would always end with a high-pitched declaration: 'My name is Gauhar Jaan!' The need for such a declaration was critical, since the recordings were sent to Hanover, Germany, to press and the statement allowed the sound engineers to recognize the artist.

In the absence of proper recording studios in those times, the recording was made in a temporary studio in two opulent hotel rooms in Calcutta. As previously mentioned, these records were then produced in Germany and sent back to India.

Gauhar proved to be a great influence in promoting the gramophone in India, where locals had little to no curiosity for western music. She also promoted interest in Indian classical music, which had until then been only enjoyed by those who could afford private mehfils.

By 1903, her albums began to appear in the Indian markets and were in great demand, understandably earning her the title—'The Gramophone Girl'. In her ensuing illustrious

---

with a high rotational speed that could yield up to 30 minutes of playing time per side.

musical journey, she went on to record up to 600 songs in more than 10 languages, including but not limited to English, French and even Pashto.

She was not constrained to one genre of music and was equally talented in the Dhrupad style of singing along with thumris, *dadras*, *kajris*, *horis*, *taranas*, Rabindra sangeet and even bhajans. Her popular thumri, 'Raske Bhare Tore Nain' continues to mesmerize audiences with her melancholic rendition of the timeless composition set to Raga Bhairavi.

Her prominence rose to such levels that her photographs appeared on several photo postcards and even on matchboxes manufactured all the way in Austria. In addition to her musical skills, her remarkable good looks, glamorous lifestyle, fluency in many languages and dialects and her ability to articulate Urdu and Hindi verses proficiently, made her a prominent name both domestically and internationally.

She had the extraordinary privilege of singing in front of Emperor George V at the iconic Delhi Durbar in 1911 where she performed 'Mubarak Ho Yeh Jalsa Tajposhi Ka', alongside Janki Bai of Allahabad. At this historic ceremony, with the Emperor, Queen and all the Indian princes in attendance, Gauhar Jaan, along with Janki Bai, were ushered to the Emperor post the performance. There, he praised both the singers for their skills and presented them with a 100 guineas as an expression of his appreciation.[8]

∽

[8]Sampath, Vikram, 'The Romance of Gauhar Jaan', *Mint*, 16 April 2010, https://tinyurl.com/2f9ey6jv. Accessed on 27 January 2023.

With such soaring success, soon Gauhar Jaan was drenched in fame, riches and luxuries that few can imagine even today. As it often happens with the ultra-rich, she developed several habits to flaunt her hard-earned riches. She was exceptionally fond of her pets, especially her cat.

Gauhar became famous (or rather infamous) for the way she boasted about her riches and influence. One of the most interesting examples of this was when she had apparently squandered ₹1,200 to mark her cat's wedding. Another story is about the time she spent ₹20,000 for a celebration because her cat had a litter of kittens.[9] In another instance of her extravagance, after she had been convinced by a patron to go to Datia to perform in a soirée, she demanded her very own train, wherein her entire coterie of chefs, assistant aides, private *hakeem*, *dhobi*, barber and scores of subordinates went along. It is evident that Gauhar was a prima donna in those times.

Gaisberg observed that whenever Gauhar arrived to record, she would always wear the finest jewels and clothes. He also noted how she never appeared to sport the same jewellery twice.[10]

Gauhar had a peculiar obsession with cars and royal wagons. She was very keen on the idea of horse racing and used to take a trip to Bombay during racing season. Such

[9]Sampath, Vikram, 'Gauhar Jaan, India's First Record Artist, Took Rs 3,000 a Session & Threw Parties for Her Cat', *The Print*, 5 May 2019, https://tinyurl.com/m4p7uy56. Accessed on 27 January 2023.

[10]Sen, Indrajit, 'Gauhar Jaan of Calcutta-The First to Record Hindustani Classical Music on Gramophone in India', *GetBengal.com*, https://tinyurl.com/ukd6anj4. Accessed on 27 January 2023.

was her love for racing that she would often flout the state regulations in Calcutta and go around in her horse-driven wagon for which she also paid a fine of ₹1,000 a day to the Viceroy (only the Viceroy was allowed to have a horse-driven wagon in those days). Even though the government warned her to avoid breaking the law, she continued to live her life the way she pleased.

Gauhar Jaan's popularity grew to a level only few women during that time could imagine. A few records have indicated that she became a *crorepati* by the early twentieth century[11], but the sheer enormity of her fortune can never be known.

∽

By the early twentieth century the freedom movement was at its peak in India. The British were unrelenting and so were the Indian freedom fighters. No stone was left unturned to gain momentum in freeing the nation from the clutches of the cruel foreign power. The world of courtesans and tawaifs was intrinsically entangled with the Indian society at that time.

Mahatma Gandhi requested Gauhar Jaan to extend her support to the struggle for independence. Gandhi's close friend, Triloki Nath Aggarwal, in his biography, has said:

When Gandhiji was collecting donations for Swaraj Aandolan, he requested Gauhar, too, to donate something. She readily agreed. But on one condition, that Gandhiji would come to see her performance, the earnings of which she would donate. Gandhiji too

---

[11]'Gauhar Jaan', *Indpaedia.com*, https://tinyurl.com/5xbfbwjz. Accessed on 27 January 2023.

agreed. But on the day of her performance, Gandhiji had some urgent political work to attend to. So he asked Maulana Shaukat Ali to collect the donation from her the next day.[12]

The courtesan community at large was brushed off this way very often. This was when the prominent *baijis* and tawaifs of Gauhar's times formed a group and requested to join and contribute towards the non-cooperation movement. Congress refuted this request outright. Even when Gandhi met a group of courtesans in Barisal (in present-day Bangladesh), who expressed their desire to join the Indian National Congress, Gandhi urged them to start spinning the *charkha* instead. In an editorial in *Young India*, his weekly publication, he stated, 'I am firmly of the opinion that, so long as they continue the life of shame, it is wrong to accept donations or services from them or to elect them as delegates or to encourage them to become members of the Congress.'[13]

Even though tawaifs were an intrinsic part of the Indian society at that time, they still lived at the fringes of the society and were especially looked down upon by the upper class gentry. It is evident that the non-cooperation movement was not the non-discrimination movement.

∽

[12]'Gauhar Jaan: The Most Famous "Tawaif" of British India', *National Herald*, 26 June 2018, https://tinyurl.com/59twprkm. Accessed on 27 January 2023.

[13]Rao, Soumya, 'Tawaifs: The Unsung Heroes of India's Freedom Struggle', *Prism*, 20 June 2019, https://tinyurl.com/2bavya9u. Accessed on 22 March 2023.

There are many iconic anecdotes about Gauhar Jaan. Similar to many iconic figures, it is mostly impossible to discern between fact and fiction when it comes to her life. Along those lines, there is one striking anecdote concerning the well-known baiji, Benazir.

Apparently, Benazirbai was once at a mehfil performing in front of the great Gauhar. Benazirbai was adorned in all her ostentatious jewels. After Benazir's performance, Gauhar addressed the young baiji and said that while her jewels may shine in bed, at a mehfil, her music has to do the job. After saying this, Gauhar Jaan rendered a remarkable public performance.

Young Benazir was embarrassed and when she met Gauhar later in Bombay, she offered all her jewels as an apology to her tutor, who took her in and trained her in refined classical *taleem*. After 10 years of intense practice, Benazirbai is said to have had the chance to perform again in front of Gauhar. This time it is said that Gauhar came to Benazir and courteously declared that her voice was really sparkling now.

As a courtesan of repute, Gauhar Jaan had her own status and style. In the 1920s, the Indian elites, equipped with western education, protested against tawaif culture and approached the Viceroy to prohibit it. As a response, Gauhar famously commented that the Viceroy should be mindful of his own business as his annual salary was equal to what she got for a single mujra. Along with being a scholar and a musician, Gauhar was also a powerful, brave and lively woman.

Once, when it was forbidden for Indians to wander or drive on the street between 5.00 p.m. to 9.00 p.m., Gauhar was seen racing in her famous Fitton car. The British patrol officer, mistaking her for a British lady, first waved at her. But as soon as he was informed that she was an Indian, he rushed to her and ordered her to pay a fine of ₹500. Gauhar looked very closely at him, caressed his chin and proclaimed, 'Oh, you are so good looking. I would have given you a thousand bucks in tip,' she said. She then flipped out ₹500 at him and drove off.[14]

∽

The private life of any public figure becomes problematic on close examination and Gauhar Jaan's was no different. When it comes to her romantic liaisons, there were three significant men. One of them was the Bengali zamindar, Nimai Sen. The essence of his affection for her was shown by the excessive and expensive presents he bestowed upon Gauhar. While tawaifs were especially famed for receiving significant material gifts from their patrons, even by these standards, this degree of material admiration was exceptional.

Another important partnership in her life was with Abbas, who was her assistant and used to accompany her on the table. Gauhar got married to him even though he was 10 years younger than her. This arrangement soured once she became aware of his unfaithfulness. He, in turn, wrapped her up in a long string of litigations.

Another relationship of hers with Amrit Keshav Nayak, a well-known Gujarati stage performer. It is said that the relationship lasted three to four years. Gauhar, who had

[14]'Gauhar Jaan: The Most Famous "Tawaif" of British India', *National Herald*, 26 June 2018, https://tinyurl.com/59twprkm. Accessed on 27 January 2023.

pined for love, finally found her true partner in him. The relationship is believed to have been stable and harmonious, however, sadly it ended with her partner's unexpected death. What remains of his memory is Gauhar's evergreen album, a *dadra* composed by him, which the artists had composed together in Raga Ghara. This tragic incident broke Gauhar and she turned into a shadow of herself.

∽

Gauhar Jaan's life was shrouded in scandal right from her birth. Her immense wealth became her biggest enemy. It seems that, through the beginning of the twentieth century, she was entangled in one litigation or another. All of these were pertaining to men who wished to leech on the wealth she had created through her own hard work. Even her ancestry, traced back to an Armenian heritage, has been spoken about a lot and there have been findings and debates regarding her birth.

In the 1911 inheritance court case, Gauhar Jaan was contested by a supposed brother who tried to claim to inherit the property of her mother, Malka Jaan. Gauhar Jaan's opponent, was a man named Bagaloo. He claimed that he, not Gauhar, was the rightful heir of Malka Jaan. He subsequently argued that as legal heir, he ought to have the right to her entire inheritance. He went on to explain, though, that if Gauhar was confirmed to be the daughter of Malka Jaan, he should be given half of the estate. It was during this case that Gauhar found and brought her father to the court to give a testimony regarding her birth.

The formal court proceedings finally made Gauhar's father publicly accept her, albeit forcefully. It so happened that when the court, chaired by Justice A.N. Chaudhuri, asked William to clarify his ancestry to nullify the claims made by Bagaloo, the court discovered how William had mixed up his father and grandfather's names while registering Gauhar's birth certificate. A.N. Chaudhuri, thus, quoted in his ruling: 'In connection with the statement he [Robert] made on Wednesday regarding his father's name, he mixed up his grandfather's name with his father's name. Where he should have given his father's name he gave his grandfather's name. Ellen Angelina was the name of his daughter.'[15]

Although her birthright to the estate as the daughter of Malka Jaan was proved, the flaky recounting of her father's own heritage put her lineage in question. Nonetheless, she won that particular case.

However, the case filed by Abbas proved to be particularly damaging for her. It seems despite all the popularity and adoration, Gauhar Jaan pined for romantic happiness her entire life. Abbas must have sensed this vacuum in Gauhar's life and the fact that she was a childless millionaire would have certainly edged him forward to propose marriage. Gauhar accepted and got married to Abbas, oblivious of her husband's sinister intentions. Once married, Abbas went on splurging Gauhar Jaan's hard-earned wealth, lavishly spending it on his mistresses.

Once Gauhar became aware of Abbas' embezzlement and infidelity, she wanted nothing more to do with him. Gauhar Jaan won the lawsuit that Abbas had filed to stake a

---

[15]Chater, Liz, 'The Story of Gauhar Jaan', *The Daily Star*, 8 August 2020, https://tinyurl.com/3yteyrws. Accessed on 27 January 2023.

claim to her estate, but she depleted her assets while financing her high-profile attorneys. It would not be too far a stretch to state that Gauhar was driven and pressured by difficult circumstances, just because she became an excessively rich courtesan. In comparison to her days of being a celebrity, after this case, Gauhar Jaan was diminished to near poverty.

ᘒ

Gauhar Jaan moved around quite a bit in her later years. Initially, she was a court singer in the princely court of Darbhanga, then she moved to Rampur and was appointed as a court singer there. Thereafter, she moved to Bombay for a brief period. Ultimately, at the behest of King Krishna Raja Wadiyar IV, she moved to the royal palace of Mysore.

At the age of 55, she was declared the court musician of Mysore.[16] This appointment, however, did not last long. She passed away on 17 January 1930, before she turned 57. Her final days in Mysore could not have been described as happy. She was essentially isolated. Over time, the legal threats of her ex-husband as well as her conniving family and relatives diminished the riches she had once accumulated.

It is tragic and ironic that a millionaire who once didn't flinch at paying a ₹500 fine, was later reduced to receiving a humble pension from the Maharaja of Mysore. She was also in ill health. She breathed her last, almost penniless, at the age of 56. It is often said that the famous Begum Akhtar was interested in pursuing a career in Hindi movies in her earlier

---

[16]'Google Doodle Honours Gauhar Jaan: Who Was She?', *India Today*, https://tinyurl.com/2tcyufd8. Accessed on 27 January 2023.

years but after hearing the mellifluous singing of Gauhar and her mother Badi Malka Jaan, she gave up the idea entirely and dedicated herself to studying Indian classical music.

It must be acknowledged that Gauhar Jaan holds credit for creating a three-minute structure for classical presentations. At a time when Indian classical music was limited to the courts and residences of the ultra-elite, it was Gauhar who made it open to the general populace by capturing her melodies on the gramophone, going on to become a phenomenon across India. She recorded in various languages, including Bengali, Hindustani, Gujarati, Tamil, Marathi, Arabic, Persian, Pashto, French and English. She unknowingly altered the direction of Indian music in this pursuit.

The way she was pushed into oblivion in the final period of her life is very unfortunate. After her death, she was buried in an unmarked grave, as an epitaph would have burned a huge hole in the pocket of her tight-fisted host. She was an enigmatic character during her glamorous days, but the mystique of her life has not necessarily ended with her passing. She was the queen of the divas of her times. Even today, few stars can match the glitz and glamour with which she lived her fabulous life. Gauhar Jaan wasn't just an artist—she was an era.

7

JANKI BAI

The Courtesan on a Knife's Edge

A thing of beauty is a joy forever: its loveliness
increases; it will never pass into nothingness.[1]

In the early twentieth century, in present-day Allahabad, the
British colonial rule over India was growing. At the same
time, the high society of Awadh had continued to flourish.
A star was rising in the city where musicians, performers
and poets often gathered together. This star had pronounced
cheekbones; a broad, dusky face; a powerful, wide Mongolian
nose; and a sculpted, lidded appearance. She adorned a lot
of silver strings, lockets and necklaces. With humongous,
jewelled danglers hanging heavily on her earlobes and
elaborate diaphanous drapes wrapping her girthy frame—
she was a sight of solid affluence with an imposing presence.
This star had a matron-like appearance and was someone
who elicited intimidation.[2]

This star was Janki Bai '*Chhappan Chhuri*', who had been
stabbed 56 times in her prime, but recovered miraculously
and went on to be known for the beauty of her voice.

Janki Bai enthralled audiences everywhere she performed
and her followers included several maharajas, maharanis,
poets, prosecutors, nawabs and even public officials. She

[1]Keats, John, 'Endymion, Book I, [A Thing of Beauty Is a Joy for Ever]',
Poets.org, https://tinyurl.com/3kzr63sw. Accessed on 29 January 2023.
[2]Saran Gaur, Neelum *Requiem in Raga Janki*, Penguin Random House, 2018.

was raised in a nautch household and grew to become the goddess of Allahabad, her voice carrying her from destitution to mansions and imperial *durbars*.

∽

Janki Bai was born in Banaras in 1880. From whatever little is known about her origin, her parents were Shivbalakram and Manki. Her father, Shivbalakram, is said to have been a wrestler belonging to the Ahir community. He left his wife and daughter quite early in the marriage after falling in love with another woman.

Akin to other deserted women of that era, Manki was forced to sell her residence and move to Allahabad. She did so with the aid of a lady in Banaras, who had in actuality, slyly sold both Manki and Janki to the manager of a very well-known kotha. Over time, Manki started to run the kotha after the manager died.

Even as a kid Janki was passionate about music and her mother discovered her musical talent quite early on. It is said that Manki hired Hassu Khan of Lucknow on a regular salary of a high amount at the time as Janki's initial music education tutor. Janki was also educated and mastered several languages, including Persian, Urdu, Sanskrit and English. This knowledge definitely influenced her subsequent artistic style. Later in her career, she wrote poems and published an original collection of poetry.

The music space in that era seems to have had a lot of complex background narratives defining it. For instance, around this time male performers took a backseat in the entertainment world as the participation of women increased.

Performers like Gauhar Jaan and Janki Bai dominated the space, performed in many tongues and went on to demand a fee greater than most *ustads*. Sadly, they were cheated out of their respective fortunes by their male beaus, leaving them pride poor and shattered.

Janki getting the uncanny yet sad title of '*Chhappan Churi*' is also said to be the result of the wrath of one such jilted man. There exist plenty of unsubstantiated anecdotes about this infamous incident linked to her disfigured face. One oral tale suggests she was attacked by Lakshmi, her stepmother, who Janki had caught with her secret male partner while in the act. The most famous anecdote, however, remains of the rejected suitor. As per the tale, she was assaulted by a former patron when he was refused sexual gratification by a young Janki. One day, he simply came to the roof when Janki was all alone and ravaged her face with 56 slits using his sword-like knife.

One has to remember that in those times, a performing artist, and that too a woman, had to be pleasing to the eye, regardless of whether they were singers or dancers. They had to be the epitome of beauty, grace and elegance all woven into one. Male ustads, on the other hand, were given leeway on these high standards as is the norm in any patriarchal society. Nevertheless, even in those times Janki Bai, through sheer grit and determination, made a mark with her voice.

∽

In what must have been a grand imperial evening at the palace of the princely state of Rewa, in present-day Madhya Pradesh, the King, a true aficionado of music, was transfixed by a woman's voice.

The strength of this music and the lilting harmony of the songstress mesmerized the king. Yet, he was quite astounded that the artist had chosen to perform from behind a curtain. What sort of coquettish play was this courtesan indulging in by shielding herself from the eyes of the Maharaja of such a majestic princely state? The peeved King asked the artist to present herself to him. But Janki declined, stating that she'd risk his fury and finish the performance instead.

The enchantment of her voice had put a spell on the King. She was brilliantly lavished with precious presents and was assured that the influence of her music surpassed everything. This performance opened doors of several palaces, mansions and salons for Janki. She became a regular at the courts of Rewa, Patiala and even the Rani of Jaunpur started making annual visits to Allahabad to hear her sing. But times were changing swiftly.

Thomas Edison's invention of the phonograph (later known as gramophone) signalled the beginning of a new age in world music. This invention was taken a step further by Emile Berliner with his invention of flat discs for audio recording.

Frederick William Gaisberg was one of the pioneers of this new age of recording with relation to India. At that time, he was employed in the studios of the Gramophone Company in London. An original catalogue cites the signatures of the musicians, Dr Harnamdas, Capt. Bholanath, Hazrat and Ahmed, all of whom lived in London back then. They sang or chanted in Persian, Hindi and Urdu, but sadly none of these recordings were preserved.

In view of the great capacity of the music industry in India, the Gramophone Company established its Indian headquarters in Calcutta. In another year or two after that, Gaisberg arrived in Calcutta with his leading technical team of specialists with the sole aim to record. At this stage, they had to go to every location where the artists were performing in order to record. In under six weeks, they travelled to various parts of India and captured over 600 records.

Male singers and ustads were unsure of this new age development and the superstitious stories of gramophone recording devices capturing the souls and voices of the singers were aplenty. The male perfomers were losing their bastion and it was owing to their arrogance and illiteracy that the way was paved for the powerful voices of female singers like Janki Bai.

For female musicians in India, the gramophone was an exciting new medium of self-expression as well as profits. It also equipped them with far broader audiences and recognition unheard of at that time, since their identities and birthplaces were revealed at the end of each recording. Almost all of the musicians recorded were experienced female vocalists who were committed to the preparation needed for producing gramophone recordings. Janki Bai was among the first in those ranks.

Owing to Janki Bai's increasing popularity in music circles, the Gramophone Company chose to record her on a disc, making her one of the first women to ever do so. She was compensated with ₹250 for 20 titles during the initial recording session in 1907, a sum which went up to ₹900 for 24 titles in the subsequent year.[3] Janki also sang with many other record labels such as Megaphone Company and Hindustan Musical Products, among others. By the end of 1910, the Gramophone Company fully realized Janki Bai's status as a star performer and raised her compensation to ₹5,000 per sitting. They also attempted to enter into an exclusive agreement with her, which she ultimately declined, as she was not one to be bound.

By 1913, Janki Bai's violet-coloured gramophone music albums began to be issued.[4] The Gramophone Company usually released all their discs as black label, and though the violet label did not differ from the black in terms of quality, it was a sign of prominence given only to the top artists of those times. It was certainly an indicator of an artist's star reputation.

While she began recording for The Gramophone Company only in 1907, many believe that she was being documented by Gaisberg in his initial recording foray as well. Unfortunately, those archives have either been lost or destroyed. Between the years 1907 and 1929, she recorded more than 250 titles.[5]

Janki Bai recorded live throughout the acoustic phase, and subsequently, she also recorded with accompanying electrical instruments. Her repertoire represented her Allahabadi style, which she inherited from her mother and guru. Her recorded

---

[3]Sampath, Vikram, 'Janki Bai, Singer Disfigured by 56 Stab Wounds Sold More Records Than Her Contemporaries', *The Print*, 2 June 2019, https://tinyurl.com/2252jp5y. Accessed on 29 January 2023.
[4]Ibid.
[5]Ibid.

pieces are in a Ganga–Jamuna tehzeeb with a delectable mixture of Hindi and Urdu and mainly include *ragadaari* music and genres such as dadra, hori, kajri, chaiti, bhajan and ghazal, among others. Most of Janki Bai's recordings were done in Allahabad, Lucknow, Delhi and Calcutta.

One could almost hear her flamboyant nature when, at the very end of every album, she pronounced her identity as 'Mera Naam Janki Bai Allahabad'.[6] Amusingly, she even weaved this declaration within the notes of the ragas that she sang.

∽

The year 1911 was instrumental for both Janki Bai as well as India. With the death of King Edward VII on 6 May 1910, King George V succeeded his father. With that, the responsibilities of the crown, the title of Emperor of India and the reign of an empire fell upon him.

Traditionally, durbars were held to mark each regime change, but the Delhi Durbar of 1911 was the only one where the monarch himself would be present. Months of preparations went into welcoming him and organizing the ceremonial coronation. Many believe that King George's visit was their way of showing that, after the Mughals, they were the new masters of India. King George and Queen Mary donned their coronation robes for the durbar. The King wore a crown designed exclusively for the event, lined with over 6,000 diamonds, rubies, sapphires and other gemstones. Commemorations began on 7 December 1911 with the arrival of the King and Queen in India.

---

[6]Ibid.

A variety of events took place over the next few weeks, along with the royal couple attracting over a million guests to the Red Fort in Delhi. Proclamations were read to shift the imperial Indian capital from Calcutta to Delhi. It was a given that to memorialize such historic events, there should be celebrations like those never seen before.

Alongside Gauhar Jaan, it was Janki Bai who was requested to attend the Delhi Durbar of 1911 to sing before King George V, wherein they sang 'Mubarak Ho Yeh Jalsa Tajposhi Ka'. Janki and Gauhar shared a mutual rivalry, which is usual among divas of their stature. This was also quite evident in their dynamic while they performed, as one tried to outdo the other.

What gave Janki Bai an upper hand in this rivalrous relationship was that she was also an author and deemed herself a pupil of the Urdu writer, Akbar Allahabadi. Janki Bai even published a set of self-composed poems. She penned a really good couplet dripping in irony about the previously married and divorced Gauhar, indicating how *Khuda* had granted Gauhar Jaan all but a *shauhar*. Regardless of this rivalry, when Janki Bai and Gauhar Jaan sang, the new monarch was so impressed with their talent that he gave 100 guineas to each of them as a parting gift.[7]

Her inclusion in the imperial durbar catapulted Janki Bai to new heights of success. It is believed that the sales for many of her titles reached over 25,000 copies, something that was unheard of in those times. The record shops in Allahabad

---

[7]Sampath, Vikram, 'The Romance of Gauhar Jaan', *Mint*, 16 April 2010, https://tinyurl.com/2f9ey6jv. Accessed on 27 January 2023.

and the places surrounding it were often jam-packed with people whenever the latest shipment of her records was put up for sale. This was a clear reflection of the star status Janki Bai had achieved.

∽

As is the case with most successful artists, their art is like a jealous lover and in their real lives, they are often bereft of any genuine relationship.

Janki Bai had a chaotic, frustrating and confusing romantic life. Beginning with jilted lovers who slashed her face, she had to go through being repeatedly manipulated and exploited by her patrons. Disgusted by the grotesque nature of men, she gave up on the idea of falling in love and sought to adopt a child and find comfort through motherly love. However, this also turned out to be a disappointing choice for Janki. Her adopted son grew up to be a drunkard and a failure, unable to take care of his ageing mother.

Marred by successive disenchantments, Janki Bai's diminishing and ageing self fell in love one last time. This time, it was with a much younger man, Abdul Haq, who was already married. He was an opportunist intent on taking advantage of a rich spinster. He wished to dupe Janki Bai out of her hard-earned wealth, accumulated through years of work.

It is rather strange how the stories of rich and famous divas of that time dying in penury is almost familiar. Gauhar Jaan also died penniless, despite her distinguished recording career. Rasoolan Bai died in poverty, working at a little tea shop in front of the radio station where she was once often broadcasted. Mylapore Gauri Ammal, the last standing devadasi of the Kapaleeshwar temple of Madras (now Chennai), was cremated with money collected from others. She was in such a bad state that neither her son nor her granddaughter had money for her cremation. Even Janki Bai was left with little by the end of her life.

The broken-hearted musician subsequently resorted to charity and formed a trust for the underprivileged with her remaining earnings. The funds from this trust were used to provide needy children with the requisite economic resources to study; to arrange public gatherings for both Hindu and Muslim rituals; and to give garments to the needy during the winter season. The trust exists in Allahabad even today and is functioning in the name of Janki Bai, keeping her memory alive.

Janki Bai died alone and discontented in 1934 and was buried by acquaintances in a graveyard near the Allahabad train station. She left behind her sonorous voice in disc records for generations to hear and honour.

8

JADDAN BAI

The Mother of Mother India

Directed and produced by a woman and that woman the author of the story and script, the writer of the music and songs, as well as the singer, and to crown it all, the star of the picture India's only woman director and producer, and one of the country's famous songstresses...[1]

To be the first in any field, day or age takes immense amount of grit, determination and courage—even more so for a woman in a deeply patriarchal and patronizing society. To break the glass ceiling, such a woman must strike a blow that will astound the onlookers en masse.

This is the story of Jaddan Bai who was born to a renowned courtesan mother, Daleepa Bai. Jaddan Bai was a courtesan, lover and mother, but at heart she was a lady with an iron will. Such was Jaddan Bai's influence that by the time she passed away on 8 April 1949, she had established her stardom as one of the feistiest leading personalities in the rapidly expanding Bombay film industry.

Imperious in her mannerisms, Jaddan Bai had mastery over the very lyrical Urdu–Hindi language owing to her ganga–jamuni upbringing. Conflict resolution was her forte

[1]Mukherjee, Debashree, 'Screenwriting & Feminist Rewriting: The Lost Films of Jaddan Bai (1892-1949)', *Academia.edu*, https://tinyurl.com/yxhypz88. Accessed on 28 February 2023.

and leading producers and directors paid heed to Jaddan's advice. This spirited lady was generous to a fault and had a string of admirers.

Belonging to the tawaif culture, Jaddan was groomed into being a sophisticated courtesan who catered to the nobility of the Indian subcontinent.

ℭ

Jaddan Bai's story began in the politically bustling town of Allahabad around 1892. Legend has it that her mother, Daleepa Bai, was a child widow from a Brahmin household around an area of east Uttar Pradesh (United Provinces in late nineteenth century). It is said that she was abducted by a wandering group of Muslims who trained and managed tawaifs. A parallel story was that the child widow, Daleepa decided to marry a wandering Muslim musician, Miajaan.

As per the abduction story, it is believed that she was thoroughly and proficiently trained in the high arts that she required to become a consummate courtesan. Soon, Daleepa's singing and dancing dexterity gained her much prominence, after which her managers got her married into the community to the group's sarangi player, Miajaan.

No matter which version of the story one chooses to believe, it is evident that fate tricked her into leading a life of a renowned courtesan rather than being a widow.

Around this time, Vazir Jaan, a renowned courtesan of the United Provinces invited Daleepa Bai and her husband to reside with her in Allahabad. It is believed that in another part of the same *haveli* resided the scion of the Nehru family—Pandit Motilal Nehru.

Thus began a twisted tale of fate intertwining the first political family of India with the soon-to-be first cinematic family of the nation. It is popularly believed that Daleepa Bai was well acquainted with the Nehru family and that her daughter, Jaddan, had even tied rakhi to Jawaharlal Nehru.

Ashok Kumar, the yesteryear actor, has observed that Jaddan often wrote letters to Indira Gandhi.[2] Jaddan Bai and Indira Gandhi's friendship was one forged between two strong women of similar character through a long intertwined family history.

౭

Jaddan herself, although involved with various men in her lifetime, was legally married only once. Her eldest child, Akhtar Hussain, was a son from her liaison with a Gujarati Hindu businessman, Narottamdas Khatri, when she was 17. Her second liaison with the harmonium master, Ustad Irshad Meer Khan, also ended after he sired Anwar Hussain.

Mohanchand Uttamchand, from a well-to-do family in Rawalpindi, was the third man in her life. He had intentions to study medicine and become a doctor, for which he was to go to England. But after meeting Jaddan and getting absolutely entranced by her beauty and character, he fell in love with her and proposed marriage.

Mohan babu's family was miffed with him and threatened to break all ties if he went ahead and married a woman four years older than him, who was already a mother of two and

[2]Sharma, Sampada, 'Sunil Dutt Fell in Love with Nargis as She Took Care of His Ill Sister: "I Knew She Was the One"', *The Indian Express*, 1 June 2022, https://tinyurl.com/2t6k3pkt. Accessed on 30 January 2023.

whose profession was believed to lead men into scandalous alleys. Nonetheless, he braved the consequences of going against his family to tie the knot with Jaddan Bai.

However, almost like the recurrent plot twists in a movie, Mohan's troubles were not over yet. Jaddan was ready for the marriage only if he embraced Islam. This conversion was done by none other than the great freedom fighter—Maulana Abul Kalam Azad. Mohan became Abdul Rashid and the nikah took place. Although now an Islam convert, Mohan Babu also gave a Hindu name to his bride—Jayadevi.

Both husband and wife elegantly balanced the two religions and even brought up their children with a mixed religious background. As a result of this union, on 1 June 1929, Fatima Rashid was born. She went on to become the superstar actress of the Hindi film industry—Nargis. This name is a derivative of the daintily beautiful narcissus flower.

∽

Young Jaddan was groomed from an early age by her mother into the sophisticated tawaif culture. This was still a matrilineal profession with mothers passing on the skills of the trade to their daughters and training them in the arts of music, dance and poetry. It was Daleepa's training that later film helped her daughter tread into the male dominated film industry. Jaddan Bai led by example and became a singer, actress, producer, director, screenwriter and a composer. She did all of this with the label of being a proficient tawaif firmly attached to her identity.

In her initial days as a tawaif, Jaddan struggled to find her footing. Miajaan's passing away when she was five and her mother's intermittent travel across northern India (from Punjab Provinces to Chilbila village in Allahabad) led to young Jaddan only getting amateur training in the craft of vocal rendition. It is essential to remember that in the late nineteenth century, courtesans were one of the few sources of entertainment for the elite. A courtesan was expected to allure her patrons and the entire mehfil through her sonorous voice, cutting across every heart and capturing the souls of her seekers.

To this end, Jaddan Bai decided to gain formal training in Hindustani classical music or what was then known as *pukka gana*. She reached out to Shrimant Ganpat Rao, popularly known as Bhaiyya Ganpatrao, to get this training.

After his death, she advanced her musical training under Ustad Moinuddin Khan, who is renowned as one of the best thumri artists till date. Ustad Chaddu Khan Saheb, Ustad Laab Khan Saheb and Ustad Barkat Ali Khan further polished the skills of this young enchantress. She was trained in the performing arts in which the tawaifs of Allahabad, Lucknow, Calcutta and Lahore were experts. Isn't it ironic that a girl who initially could not blossom due to her inexperience in musical training, later became the first ever woman music director in the country?

Post her training, Jaddan Bai became extremely capable and resourceful in her music but she could not stick with her mother's profession in the end. This was owing to the late commencement of her training and socio-economic reasons.

This was the time when patronage for courtesans was steadily diminishing along with the dying world of rajas and nawabs. Owing to this, women like Jaddan Bai had little option but to reinvent themselves. The 1930s Hindi film industry retained some of its earlier democratic impulses but was veering towards the road of middle-class respectability and moral prejudice. A few discerning *gaanewalis* turned their attention to new avenues of sustenance, like the gramophone and radio. Jaddan did one better and chose cinema. She began to produce, act, sing and compose music for Hindi films.

Having succeeded in this environment on her own terms, Jaddan ensured that her daughter grew up thoroughly respectable. That may be the reason why Nargis was not taught how to sing. Those who remained gaanewalis had to suffer discrimination when the All India Radio put out a preference for married female vocalists over them. The gaanewalis were even required to use a different entrance so that their presence at recordings would not annoy 'normal', well-born employees.

Retrospectively, her entry into cinema came at a historically significant time. The early twenty-first century was when the industry began to earn some respect and women from 'respectable' households began to act in films. This was also the time when tawaifs and ostracized Anglo-Indian ladies in Calcutta were beginning to lose popularity.[3] Jaddan Bai, therefore, was like a bridge between two waves of history that changed Indian cinema forever.

ॐ

---

[3]Sen, Sudarshana, 'Living Stories of Anglo-Indian Women in Kolkata', *International Journal of Anglo-Indian Studies*, Vol. 14, No. 1, 2014, pp. 31–40.

At the age of 40, Jaddan began her career as a film actress. Hakim Ramprasad, a film producer based in Lahore, was enamoured by Jaddan and offered her a role in a major film. Jaddan Bai became a part of Playart Phototone, a film production firm, around the year 1932, and acted in her first film *Raja Gopichand* in 1933.

It is essential to remember that during this time, cinema in the Indian subcontinent was just in its nascent stage. The subcontinent had just seen its first all-singing all-talking, full-length feature film, *Alam Ara,* release in 1931. With the introduction of sound in Indian movies, many novel jobs, such as dialogue writers, dialect coaches, song writers and many more, came up. Sadly, there aren't many studio archives or production data available for South Asia's silent and nascent talkie eras. As a result, it is quite challenging to track the history of screenwriting techniques.

The introduction of sound also meant that many actresses of the silent era could no longer perform. This was due to their lack of proficiency in Hindi–Urdu and singing (as there was no concept of playback singing in those days). As a multilingual trained singer, Jaddan Bai was exactly what the industry was looking for in an actress at the time. Therefore, Jaddan Bai was cast in her debut film as the mother of the title character, Raja Gopichand, hired not for her youth but for her voice, diction and enunciation. After her debut, she worked in *Insaan Ya Shaitan, Prem Pareeksha* and *Seva Sadan.*

It is a testament to Jaddan Bai's ambition and courage that in 1933 she decided to give up her established fame and wealth in Calcutta and relocated to Bombay with the radical plan of becoming a film producer. An apartment near the posh Marine Drive area was rented and old patrons, who had taken a liking to Jaddan in her earlier days, were contacted to fund her new projects. Jaddan Bai launched her own film production company, Sangeet Movietone, in 1934. The company's first feature film *Talashe Haq* was produced in 1935.

Jaddan Bai directed as well as acted in *Talashe Haq* (1935), *Hriday Manthan* (1936), *Madam Fashion* (1936), *Jeewan Swapna* (1937) and *Moti Ka Haar* (1937). Jaddan also changed her daughter's name from Fatima to Baby Rani when she was six and made her act in *Madam Fashion*. She made the right decision for her gifted daughter and set her up for great success.

The film industry at this time provided a relatively open playing field for those with the capital to finance their own ventures. Caught between the scarcity of talented singer–actresses and the clamour for 'cultured ladies', Bombay cinema negotiated a fine balance between musical talent and camera presence. Jaddan Bai had the foresight to sense the inevitable arrival of cinema's glory days as Indian liberals got closer to power.

During the 1930s, coming across good quality screenplays was one of the major problems facing the Bombay film industry. Here is an example of a commonly held unfavourable opinion from the age: 'A better picture is only possible with a better story. With all the technique in the world, a poor and lame story cannot be dressed into a big show. [...] In India, scenarios are written by Munshis, fakirs and street minstrels. With the exception of three or four good scenario writers, we have no men for this job.'[4] This was written in 1937, six years after the debut of India's first Hindustani talkie picture, by which time the screenwriter's oeuvre had undergone a significant transformation.

The general agreement appears to indicate that women were not employed in the Bombay film industry other than as actors, dancers or junior technicians. We have access to Jaddan Bai's scripting credits mostly because she also developed and directed her original movies.

One must note that most of her films had a critical tone, assessing the degenerating moral values of a society that was deeply influenced by western moralistic ideas. Jaddan was consciously participating in the nationalist discourse and her films served as a veiled gesture of support for swadeshi values. She incorporated aspects of both western and swadeshi traditions in her personal life. An advertisement that was printed in 1932, the day before Jaddan Bai made her movie debut, talked about her groomed charms and the specific abilities that may raise her social rank. Popular 'Western' activities like tennis, swimming and driving were accorded equal weight to her swadeshi scholarly interests.

But dance, music, cinema and performing arts at large were still seen as a derogatory professions and those who practised it were by default termed as beings of low moral character. Thus, it is not a surprise that even Jaddan Bai, who was a pioneering woman in the Hindi film industry, was occasionally humiliated when her past came haunting

---

[4]Mukherjee, Debashree, 'Screenwriting & Feminist Rewriting: The Lost Films of Jaddan Bai (1892-1949)', *Academia.edu*, https://tinyurl.com/yxhypz88. Accessed on 28 February 2023.

her present. There was a relative of the renowned author, Saadat Hasan Manto, who was insulting courtesan culture in front of Jaddan Bai (not knowing who she was).

> Apa Saadat was in her element: 'God can only protect us from these women. Whoever falls into their grasp is doomed to perish in both this realm and the next. If you fall prey to these animals, you might lose your money, your health, and your good reputation. These courtesans and prostitutes, in my opinion, are the world's worst plague.' My wife and I felt humiliated, but we had no idea how to handle Apa Saadat.[5]

Jaddan Bai apparently observed this tirade with composure before revealing her identify to the embarrassed woman. When this happened, nearly 10 years had passed since Jaddan Bai's first screenplay, but the perceptions had remained the same.

∽

Once Nargis reached her adolescence, Jaddan apparently tricked her into starring in a film for her friend, Mehboob Khan. Nargis was unwilling because she was taken out of St Mary's, an elite girls' school in Bombay, to star in the film. Jaddan also allegedly put her daughter's *nath* (virginity) on the market and allowed a wealthy Muslim prince to pay handsomely for it. Cruel to our sensibilities, the act was then treated a matter of fact, like a tradition on

---

[5]Mukherjee, Debashree, 'Screenwriting & Feminist Rewriting: The Lost Films of Jaddan Bai (1892-1949)', *Academia.edu*, https://tinyurl.com/yxhypz88. Accessed on 28 February 2023.

which the courtesan culture firmly stood.

As previously mentioned, Jaddan had asked Mohan Babu to convert to her religion. In contrast, Nargis failed to make this same demand of Raj Kapoor or Sunil Dutt.

According to some oral retellings, Jaddan Bai felt compelled to withdraw Nargis from her English-medium school, since their family's economic status had worsened due to the unstable state of the film business and Nargis was obligated to take on the burden of keeping the family afloat. Nargis was a highly educated woman whose introduction to the movie business brought her a lot of fame and success. Jaddan Bai even asked Anwar Hussain, her son, to act in her movies.

Nargis's father, Mohan, had completely abandoned his desire to become a doctor in his quest to wed Jaddan, but Nargis still had similar aspirations. However, she was compelled to undertake her first adult role at the age of 14 in Mehboob Khan's movie *Taqdeer*.

Although Nargis is said to have endured social shaming from her more traditional, non-filmy contemporaries, all such misgivings were forgotten with *Taqdeer's* success. The little girl had never previously been attracted to the world of movies, unlike her mother, Jaddan Bai. Mother and daughter now started a professional collaboration that would reap rich future dividends, as Nargis would one day become one of Hindi cinema's most beloved superstars and a respectable icon.

Jaddan was the primary breadwinner for a family of five. Even though Mohan babu was devoted to his wife, he was not equipped for any specialized profession and remained dependent on her financially. This lasted until her daughter joined in to shoulder the family's hardships.

Jaddan Bai was friends with Mehboob Khan, one of India's most successful film-makers and the one who gave Nargis her famous part in *Mother India*. He was one of the regulars at Château Marine (Jaddan's Bombay apartment), where he would sit and talk about various aspirations and initiatives.

Jaddan and her son, Akhtar, were overjoyed about Nargis's success, as there would be a star in the house and their money problems would also be gone. There were usually more than 30 dependent members[6] in Jaddan Bai's house (including the domestic workers) and only one contributing member. Nargis could now be a co-provider.

The grand man of Indian cinema, Raj Kapoor shared an interestingly complex love-hate relationship with Jaddan Bai whom he addressed as 'Bibiji'. Raj Kapoor in his film *Bobby* makes the heroine (Dimple Kapadia) open the door of her house for the hero (Rishi Kapoor) with a flour-smeared forehead, as she is alone in the house frying *bhajiyas*. This is actually how Raj Kapoor and Nargis had their first interaction, which soon blossomed into a deep love affair and became the talk of the entire town.[7]

At that time, Raj Kapoor was married with kids and

---

[6]Desai, Kishwar, '"Not Very Beautiful but Vivacious": How Nargis Was Cast in Her Breakthrough Movie "Taqdeer"', *Scroll.in*, 1 June 2017, https://tinyurl.com/3txfehe9. Accessed on 30 January 2023.

[7]'Did You Know That Rishi Kapoor-Dimple Kapadia's This Scene in "Bobby" Was Real Life Scene of Raj Kapoor and Nargis?', *The Times of India*, 14 December 2018, https://tinyurl.com/3fv2rnfn. Accessed on 30 January 2023.

Nargis was just 17. Jaddan Bai was not too happy with this liaison. In one of his interviews, Raj Kapoor has stated how Jaddan Bai, not too keen on letting Nargis and his proximity deepen, did not permit RK Films to take Nargis to Kashmir for an outdoor shoot.[8] Such was the stubborn character of Jaddan that Raj Kapoor had to relent and shoot the entire sequence in Mahabaleshwar instead. In fact, the whole family was so against the Raj–Nargis relationship that her brothers tried to get her married to the then upcoming Pakistani politician, Zulfikar Ali Bhutto, at one point.[9]

In the end, not foreseeing a steady future with a married man, Nargis broke up with Raj Kapoor. In the end, she married Sunil Dutt who, just like her father, was a Mohyal Brahmin whose family had relocated to India after the Partition.

It is interesting that Jaddan was against Nargis becoming Raj Kapoor's second wife. Maybe Jaddan Bai was seeking some respectability in society and did not want her daughter to live the life that she had.

∽

Jaddan took her last breath in the presence of Nargis and her other children on 8 April 1949. Indian culture since classical times has always acknowledged the presence of women

---

[8]Pandya, Sonal, '70 Years of Raj Kapoor's Barsaat: How the Intense Love Story Established RK Films', *Cinestaan*, 22 April 2019, https://tinyurl.com/mr44v3v2. Accessed on 30 January 2023.
[9]Bhandari, Bhupesh, 'A Family in Films & Politics', *Business Standard*, 5 February 2013, https://tinyurl.com/yc38hprs. Accessed on 30 January 2023.

who were repositories of tehzeeb, tameez, arts, dance, music, poetry and culture. It was the deceitful propaganda of the colonial masters, who wished to diminish any sense of pride and cultural identity, among Indians that led to the banishment of the traditional courtesans and artists (including weavers, painters, poets, musicians) to the fringes. There was a need for someone like Jaddan Bai to break the shackles and bring in a revolution, however subtle it might have been. The life story and career graph of Jaddan Bai reads like a timeless film script.

She was, by and large, an iron lady who ran both her household and her profession (whether as a courtesan or a film-maker) by a strict code, kept challenging herself and her character show like heated gold when challenged. The story of this lady deserves greater recognition than the history of Indian cinema has given her.

She was a woman of talent, wise business acumen and entrepreneurial spirit. As a wife and mother, she led a content life with Mohan babu and her three children and made a name for herself in an industry that was inhospitable to women. Such was the life of this remarkable courtesan.

9

BEGUM AKHTAR

The Lament of a Songstress

Divana banana hai to divana bana de
Varna kahin taqdir tamasha na bana de
Ai dekhne vaalo mujhe hans hans ke na dekho
Tum ko bhi mohabbat kahin mujh sa na bana de
Main dhūndh raha huun meri vo shama kahan hai
Jo bazm ki har cheez ko parvana bana de
Divana banana hai to divana bana de
Varna kahin taqdir tamasha na bana de[1]

(If you want me to be madly in love, turn me into a
lunatic
Otherwise the fates may turn me into a spectacle
Oh you people of the World, don't laugh at my plight
Otherwise being in love might make you like me
I am searching where my flame is beloved
That which turns everyone in the gathering into a lover
If you want me to be madly in love, turn me into a
lunatic
Otherwise the fates may turn me into a spectacle)

A voice drenched in pain emanates out of an old gramophone
and one is lost in the decadent world of ghazals—especially
the ghazals of Begum Akhtar. Her personal life encapsulates

---

[1]Lakhnavi, Behzad, 'Diwana Banana Hai to Diwana Bana De', *Rekhta.org*,
https://tinyurl.com/bdf6mjc6. Accessed on 30 January 2023.

how one's voice can drip with *viraha* when one's heart aches for music.

We've heard many older women and many older movies echo lines like, 'My *nanand* won't approve of my smoking.' Sentiments like these encompass the essence of an upper middle class Indian family in the late twentieth century. This was a time when the wives were still asked to stay in purdah and were hemmed into a dreadful silence by their parents-in-law. The line above perfectly encapsulates a generic faceless woman whose personality has been molded as per her parents-in-laws' choices. You may be surprised to know that even the star ghazal vocalist, Begum Akhtar, followed these kind of traditional notions. She was known to be ultra-fashionable for her times with her swanky new cars, shimmering jewels and elegant cigarette holders.

The famed *gayika* of the dying courtesan era chose the trappings of married life over that of films, glamour, fast cars, smoking and even music.

Begum Akhtar was known by many names in her initial years of popularity: Akhtari, Akhtari Bai, Akhtari Bai Faizabadi and so forth. Her life was akin to that of a tragic novel; she composed poetry filled with the pain of betrayal, separation and even near death. But what kept her alive was the elusive elixir of musical notes.

∽

Akhtari Bai Faizabadi was born on 7 October 1914 in the Faizabad district, Uttar Pradesh. Back then, she was just Bibi, a girl with a twinkle in her eye who was yet to fulfil her tragic destiny of heartaches and betrayal before becoming one of the most famous ghazal singers in the world. Her mother, Mushtari Bai, was a renowned courtesan of her time who married Asghar Hussain, a civil court lawyer, to become his second wife.

Akhtari Bai was born in tumultuous times, both politically and in terms of gender stereotyping in performing arts. The British, through their deep-rooted Christian sensibilities, had tainted all performing arts as being a facade for sex work.

These 'reformists' viewed the women performers as mere sex workers and wished to 'rescue' them from the clutches of these age-old 'demonic' traditions. What they did not realize was the fact that courtesan culture was a part of high art and did not require rescuing, rather it needed patronage and support. The long-standing courtesan culture was on a steep decline and women performers of that time were forced to bind themselves in a marriage to attain any sense of respectability. Even then, the past of many women continued to haunt them, so much so, that entry of courtesans was forbidden by the All India Radio in those times. This was also why Mushtari Bai, Akhtari's mother relented to Asghar Hussain's marriage proposal and agreed to leave the world of performance for good. But that was not to be.

Suspicious of Mushtari Bai's past and the real parentage of Akhtari and her twin sister, Asghar mercilessly fed poisoned *balushahi* to the twins when they were four. In an unconscious state, Akhtari and her sister were brought to the hospital but alas, her sister had already lost the battle.

Akhtari, when she woke up, asked her mother about her sister. Mushtari Bai could not bring herself to tell this four-year-old how her sister was dead and how their father had abandoned them. In retrospect, maybe it was in this very moment that Mushtari Bai resolved that the fate that befell her would not be faced by her only surviving daughter. She resolved to make her daughter independent of the frills of married life, and thus began Akhtari's training in the art of music under some of the finest maestros of her time. Mushtari Bai's resolve helped her daughter live independently without a loving father.

Later in life, she came across her father when she was performing at a *walima* in Lucknow. That evening, she found herself thinking about how proudly he introduced his other children in the reception. Out of malice, she purchased a house right in front of his. She had desired to see him all her life, but this experience had left her disenchanted forever.

Thus started Akhtari's lifelong struggle with a false sense of respectability and her quest to achieve her musical destiny.

Taken advantage of by both patrons and gurus and begetting a child while being a teenager herself—the life of the Mallika-e-Ghazal was fraught with trauma. Her childhood and teen years, it seems, were just a glimpse of this never-ending saga of pain. Perhaps, it was this drape of moroseness that brought out the heart-wrenching pain in her honeydew voice.

Akhtari started her musical training right from the tender age of seven. She was first attracted to music when she heard the songs of a renowned courtesan of her time, Chandra Bai. Her mother, however, thought it a better proposition to commence her training under Ustad Imdad Khan of the Patna Gharana.

Ustad Imdad Khan, though not a vocalist himself, was a class act in terms of playing the sitar and an exacting teacher when it came to training the young Akhtari. Once initiated into the world of Indian classical music (which in those times was known as pakka gana), Akhtari went on to receive training from Ata Mohammed Khan of Patiala.

Her quest to find an inspiration took her to Calcutta where she trained under Mohammad Khan and then on to Lahore, where the classical music stalwart of the Kirana Gharana, Ustad Abdul Wahid Khan, furthered her training. Finally, her advanced training concluded under Ustad Jhande Khan.

After this, she was thought to be prepared to take the world of Indian music by storm. However, Mushtari Bai wanted a 'respectable' life for her daughter—away from music, dancing and films, for she knew the dark alleys this profession led to. This thirst for respect would also follow Akhtari later in her life but at that time, she was on a quest to learn music. With her uncle's help, she had convinced her mother to let her pursue it as a career.

Out of all her trainings, her time with Ustad Imdad Khan were most memorable for her, especially when he guided her to explore Raga Kamod. Though she pursued it with much interest, in her heart, Akhtari was enchanted by folk tunes (like thumri, chaiti, dadra, tappa), rather than the restrictive raga form.

Another moment-that had a lasting impression on her was when she was training under Ustad Ata Mohammed Khan of Patiala around the year 1923. Her guru would make her practise in the *kharaj bharan* endlessly, which would make her quite restless.

But then one fine morning, just like that, she felt enchanted to be in the grip of music forever. She was introduced to the intricacies of Raga Gunkali which intrinsically is a very nostalgic set of *swaras*. Perhaps, this raga struck some deep chord of pain and separation within Akhtari that she then became a dedicated pupil of music, practising for hours on end.

Little did she know at the time that this dedication was about to open the doors of stardom for her soon.

∽

In 1927, in pursuit of better opportunities, the mother–daughter duo migrated to Calcutta, which was the music capital at that time. They, together with their guru, Ustad Ata Mohammed Khan, rented a house on Ripon Street. The young Akhtari was wide-eyed and entranced witnessing the big names of music soirées like Gauhar Jaan, Malka Jaan and many more right in front of her eyes. But mere inspiration was not enough to make ends meet. Possessions were getting sold and finances were getting tighter day by day when the 1934 Nepal–Bihar earthquake happened.

To collect funds for the resettlement of those hit by the earthquake, there was a huge fundraiser concert held in Calcutta. Akhtari Bai was also part of the line up for this event. Her premiere concert was held in Alfred Theatre in 1934, where her guru, Ustad Ata Mohammed Khan, began her first stage show with the ghazal:

Tuney butey harjai kuch aisi ada payee
Takta teri surat har ek tamashayee[2]

(I wish you were not a deceiver; such a quality you have got
Stares at you, yet another admirer)

Sarojini Naidu, the great Indian freedom fighter, poetess and arts patron heard Akhtari for the first time in that concert and was completely mesmerized. She not only appreciated this singer but also directed her towards singing ghazals, which later became Akhtari's lifetime quest.

Although Akhtari had been coaxed to record her voice for the newly invented disc, she was still apprehensive and, some might say, even superstitious about the device. After the concert, inspired by the kind words of Sarojini Naidu, Akhtari felt comfortable enough to go ahead and cut her first disc, which was a collection of dadras and ghazals, for the Megaphone Record Company and then for the famed HMV (His Master's Voice) label.

'Woh Asire-Daam-e-Bala', one of Akhtari's first ghazals, was soon in vogue and catapulted her into stardom. The wealthy landowners and the growing business elite were also supporters of classical music and courtesans specializing in light classical styles, such as thumri, tappa, chaiti, *baramasa* and ghazal.

Another major hit of hers was the ghazal 'Divana Banana

---

[2]Bajaj, Puja, 'The First Time Begum Akhtar Performed a Ghazal, She Ended the Performance Saying, "Mera Naam Akhtari Bai Faizabadi Hai"', *Aaj Tak*, 7 October 2017, https://tinyurl.com/khtea558. Accessed on 30 January 2023.

Hai To Divana Bana De', and there is a spiritual tale behind the success of this piece of art. Mushtari Bai was getting restless, as Akhtari, though now famous, was yet to receive the spoils of fame as much as her mother would have liked. So, Mushtari Bai took the reins in her own hands and took Akhtari to a *pir baba* in Bareilly. It is said that when Akhtari met the mendicant, he asked what bothered her. To this, she expressed her dissatisfaction with her own musical talents. The holy man asked for the notebook in which she used to jot down her favourite lyrics. He turned the pages and stopped at Behzad Lakhanavi's ghazal, 'Divana Banana Hai', and told her to sing it for her next programme.

Mushtari Bai went a step ahead and got a disc cut out of Akhatri's rendition of the ghazal and it went on to become a platinum disc, a major success. Akhtari became one of the pioneering women singers who left the decadent ambience of salons and went on to sing for public concerts. Her fame soared to such heights that she came to be known as the Mallika-e-Ghazal. Akhtari's life was now on the high road to fame and riches but tragedy, her constant friend, was about to meet her at the next turn.

Akhtari Bai embodied the rapidly dying feudal and aristocratic high culture of that time. This culture was resplendent with poetry, decadent evenings of music and dance and the hereditary tawaif culture, to which Akhtari was one of the last links. As mentioned earlier, she lived in an unsettling time for the arts at large. The British and certain Indian elites viewed Indian performing arts as lewd.

The belief system of these 'reformists' emerged from their deep-rooted western religious sentiments and philosophy, but certain regular incidents added fuel to the flame of abolising the arts.

Akhtari had a daughter named Shamima. Mushtari Bai, in order to protect Akhtari from social persecution, instructed her to tell everyone that Shamima was her sister, not her daughter. Mushtari had devised a plan to explain the existence of this newborn girl as hers. One cannot imagine the pain that Akhtari would have had to live through for years.

❦

Disillusioned with the life of a singer, Akhtari turned into a recluse, until she was beckoned back to music by a new technological advancement called talkies. One must remember that the earliest films were recorded live, much like concerts, and Akhtari's mellifluous voice along with her petite frame and doe-eyed look gave stiff competition to many of her contemporaries and rendered her a lucrative investment for film houses.

East India Film Company was scouting for a new face for their imminent projects when they stumbled upon Akhtari and found her to be perfect for the roles. Thus, she acted in two of their films *Nal Damyanti* and *Ek Din Ka Badshah*.

The world would not allow this charismatic voice to be forgotten and out of the blue came the famous director–producer, Mehboob Khan, at her doorstep. This was the same man who also had a tryst with another courtesan from this era—Jaddan Bai and her daughter Nargis, whom he presented in his award-winning film, *Mother India*.

Sensing star quality in Akhtari, Mehboob wanted to cast her for the role of 'Darling' in his upcoming film, *Roti*, which had an anti-capitalist plot and needed a bright-eyed seductress representing the trappings of a wealth-driven world. The role needed someone who could sing as well and thus, Akhtari was cast with much approval from her mother, who was now happy to see her daughter out of the clutches of anonymity, making a name for herself. But even then, Akhtari's struggles relentlessly followed her into her professional life. Mehboob Khan had originally recorded six of Akhtari's ghazals but due to a tiff with the producer at National Studios, he had to remove three of her songs. However, the remaining three are still available with the Megaphone Gramophone records.

Akhtari also appeared in the critically acclaimed film, *Jalsaghar,* by the legendary director, Satyajit Ray. The film did not receive its due acclaim initially but steadily went on to be regarded as one of the greatest works produced by the Indian film industry. She also appeared in *Ameena, Roop Kumari, Jawani Ka Nasha, Naseeb Ka Chakkar* and *Anaar Bala.*

∽

Those were the times when any female performer—whether they were dancers, singers or even actresses—were looked at with suspicion, as the world of performing arts had become decadent and hit rock bottom. The then high-society women were supposed to strictly be in purdah, let alone sing or dance in front of strangers.

However, several women of high-born status had a courtesan mother with a legitimate father from high society. Akhtari was one such exception. Even so, the

British government and its supporters were not very keen to entertain any unmarried female singer.

All India Radio would not admit women unless they were of a respectable stature or, in other words, married. In the late pre-Independence and early post-Independence era in the Indian subcontinent, to be considered respectable, one had to marry and relinquish any connections to their performing past.

By mapping Akhtari Bai's path in life and music, one can inevitably see the prevalent culture that she was still unable to shake off. Akhtari came to the musical stage when a tawaif singing was still very much a part of the upper class sociocultural scene in North India. At the peak of her singing and acting career, Akhtari decided to move back to her loving Awadh.

What better place to move to than Lucknow, the social and vibrant capital of Awadh with all its amenities and extravagances? It had its own charisma, the splendour of nawabi culture, sophisticated etiquette and courteous social graces. It was also the abode of the nobles of North India who appreciated and patronized Akhtari's *gayaki*, *andaaz* and *ada*.

Akhtari Bai bought a property in Cheena Bazaar in Lalbagh with a sophisticated salon in mind. It was an aesthetically appropriate venue for the highest echelon of Lucknow's societal structure. This house was called 'Akhtar Manzil', and in a really short time, it became a popular landmark of the city. This abode rose to fame in the early 1930s and 1940s. The attendees of this salon were the nobility and royalty of Awadh as well as far beyond.

Moved by the beauty and charm of Akhtari Bai, Raza Ali Khan could not restrain himself from gracing these mehfils and making her a court singer in the Rampur estate. But even with all the nobility at her feet, Akhtari desired what her mother never had—respect.

In those days, the only way to gain the high society's real respect was to get married. To this end, she found her partner in the young barrister, Ishtiaq Ahmed Abbasi, a member of the Talukdar family of Kakori. Abbasi Sahab was Lucknow's foremost lawyer who was popular and respected for his profession and standing in society. He had been educated in London and was a bar-at-law.

His suave looks and polished social etiquette ultimately did strike Akhtari Bai with the Cupid's arrow. After quite a secret courtship, she married Abbasi Sahab in 1945[3]. The quick ceremony raised the status of Akhtari Bai to Begum Abbasi legally and she became Begum Akhtar for her fans.

Naam Akhtar Tha, Woh Begum, Abbassi,
Tarranum unsey tha, Woh Malika-e-Tarranum[4]

(Her name was Akhtar, to him [husband] Begum Abbasi.
Melody manifested she was [for admirers], truly the
Queen of Melody)

After her wedding, Akhtari moved to Mateen Manzil, Nayagaon, the home of Abbasi's parents, until he bought a

---

[3]Khan, Hera, 'Begum Akhtar: Her Journey from a Courtesan to "Mallika-E-Ghazal"', *The Quint*, 7 October 2021, https://tinyurl.com/bdd9btj9. Accessed on 30 January 2023.
[4]Added by the author from his knowledge of Hindustani classical music

new mansion for his Begum on No. 1 Havelock Road. She strived to transform herself from a public person to a private entity, from *shama-e-mehfil baiji* to *parda-nasheen shareef zadi*.

∽

The price of respectability had to be paid—Begum Akhtar gave up music, public performances and her professional life as a concert performer.

This transformation, along with the death of her mother, pushed her into a chasm of melancholy. Since their marriage, Abbasi Sahab had prohibited his wife to sing publicly. After all, she was now an aristocrat's wife. Begum Akhtar's mental health went spiralling but she managed to survive even this extreme depression.

The day was saved thanks to Sunil Kumar Bose, the chief producer of music at the All India Radio in Lucknow, and his tenacious younger colleague, Luv Kumar Malhotra. Luv persuaded Abbasi Sahab to encourage his spouse to sing.

He refused initially but, within 10 years, a declining turn in his fortunes compelled him to let Begum Akhtar perform. Eventually, she returned elegantly to engage in what made her most delighted. Her husband stood next to her in this hour of crisis and encouraged her to restart her radio programmes and music concerts.

She began her life's second innings with greater commitment and absolute dedication, and once again managed to regain her exceptional status. Her ada and andaz defined Lucknow's nawabi opulence, she sang with a great understanding of the lyrics and she added far more to the words with her voice. She was now, once again, Mallika-e-Ghazal, Mallika-e-Tarranum and the heartbeat of millions of admirers.

She was awarded the Padma Shri in 1968 and the coveted Sangeet Natak Akademi award in 1972. She continued to garner accomplishments in her lifetime and was awarded the Padma Bhushan posthumously in 1975.

Meanwhile, her husband's estate was lost partly due to the Partition and partly due to ill management of whatever remained. But, familiar with such changes in fortune, Begum Akhtar relentlessly pursued her career and, some might say, even supported her family.

There is a very touching anecdote that is dear to everyone who knew her. The Begum used to leave a *satlarha* of tremendous value with the jewellery designer and sitarist, Arvind Parikh, during the off-season. He would, in turn, offer her money to smooth over the lean time. When the concert season started again, Begum Akhtar would give him the money in exchange for the jewellery (which was a present from the Nawab of Rampur).

This system continued for a good seven or eight years. When she passed away, the necklace was with Arvind. The gentleman and musician that he was, he returned it to the late artist's husband without asking for money in return, as he felt content enough to have been of some help to the legendary singer in her lifetime.

Always ready to lend a helping hand, in October 1974, she performed free of cost at Patkar Hall in Bombay in support of the Cancer Patients Help Society. As usual, the performance was full of elite attendance. At the end of the programme, she auctioned all the presents and artefacts she had collected and the generous amount of money from this was pledged to the cancer patients. Little did she know that this would be her last goodbye to Bombay.

Ab tumse rukhsat hoti hoon, sambhalo saaz-e-ghazal,
Naya tarana chedo, mere naghmon ko neend aati hai[5]

(I take leave of you, take care of my artful ghazals
Sing a new song, mine are drowsy with sleep)

Ahmedabad became her next success after Bombay. This programme was organized by Nilam Gamadia. It was at this programme on 27 October 1974 that the Nawab Mansoor Ali Khan Pataudi became a big admirer of hers. In the finest of courtly etiquette, she stood up courteously and presented her *adaabs* to the Nawab of Pataudi and the Bhopal aristocracy. Near the very end of this performance, she suffered a serious heart attack. The last thumri she sang in her classical style was:

Sowai nindiya jagaye...[6]

(Wake me up from slumber...)

On the evening of 30 October 1974, in Ahmedabad, she breathed her last while her beloved husband waited for her at home in Lucknow. Her casket, after many challenges, was flown from Ahmedabad to Kanpur via Delhi, and then was sent off to No. 1, Havelock Road, Lucknow.

Begum Akhtar was cremated next to her mother in

---

[5]Added by the author from his knowledge of Hindustani classical music
[6]Ibid.

Pasand Bagh, Thakurganj, as per her wishes. Thus, this elegant bird was freed from the cages of her loneliness, pain and separation forever.

> *Naam bhi leta hai ek jahan-e-rang-e-boo;*
> *Doston us naubahar-e- naaz ki batein karo;*
> *Nakhat-e-zulf-e-pareshaan, dastaan shaam-e-ghum;*
> *Subah honey tak usi andaaz ki batein karo.*[7]

---

[7]Ibid.

10

BALASARASWATI

The Last Standing Courtesan

Krishna née begane baaro
Begane baaro mukhavanne toro
Krishna née begane baaro
Kalalandige gejje, née lada bavuli
Née lavarnane natyavanaduta baaro
Krishna née begane baaro
Udiyalli udigejje, beralalli ungura
Koralalli haakida vaijayantiya maale
Krishna née begane baaro
Kasi pitambara, kaiyalli kolalu
Pusida shreegandha mayyolagamagama!
Krishna née begane baaro
Tayige bayalli jagavannu thorida
Jagadoddharaka namma udupi shri krishna
Krishna née begane baaro[1]

(With anklets in the leg and blue gem-studded bangles in
the hand,
Oh blue coloured one, come dancing to me.
In the hips you wear a belt with bells, rings on your
fingers,
And the garland of Vaijayanthi on your neck, please
come.

---

[1]'Krishnaa Nee Begane Baaro', *KarnATik*, https://tinyurl.com/78dhhbb2.
Accessed on 30 January 2023.

Adorned with yellow silk of Banaras with flute in your
hand,
And with sandal paste applied all over your body.
You who showed the universe to your mother,
Oh God who carried the earth, oh our God Udupi Sri
Krishna).

Who in all of creation has power enough to call upon God;
commanding him to hasten and appear in front of oneself,
other than a saint who has surpassed the mundane existence
of this world? Thanjavur Balasaraswati radiated this kind of
rare, divine luminosity.

Balasaraswati was awarded the Sangeet Natak Akademi
award in 1955 and the Padma Vibhushan in 1977, making
her the first female dancer in India to be decorated with the
second highest civilian award.

The famed Madras Music Academy bestowed her with
the coveted award of 'Sangeetha Kalanidhi', which was
typically reserved only for musicians. She went on to become
the only dancer ever to hold this honour.[2]

As an artist as well as a guru, she captured the spotlight
of the international dance scene. She was deemed an equal
of dancers such as Margot Fonteyn, Galina Ulanova and even
Martha Graham. But at heart Balasaraswati remained 'little
bird' (as her friends addressed her)[3], craving to relive her lost
childhood.

---

[2]Gogoi, Angarika, 'Tanjore Balasaraswati: How a Gritty Girl from TN
Took Bharatnatyam to the World', *The Better India*, 16 September 2019,
https://tinyurl.com/4m2d2e54. Accessed on 30 January 2023.
[3]Ibid.

~

In South India, Bharatanatyam was previously known by different names, such as Sadir Attam in Tamil Nadu. It was primarily performed in salons and courts, before it was popularized and deemed suitable for stage.

Classical Indian dance styles have had a lengthy and turbulent journey. The chronicled heritage of this dance practice can be traced back to more than 1,000 years. The sheer perseverance of traditional performance practitioner families in temple-driven economies was such that the style survived millennia of upheaval. Quite a few classical artists eventually came to be known as devadasis. They were known to have an intrinsically matrilineal family structure that continued to represent this art form.

Veenai Dhanammal (1867–1938) became one of those artists whose heritage in the field of entertainers can be directly traced back to over 200 years ago.

Thanjavur Balasaraswati was born in 1918 and was Veenai Dhanammal's granddaughter. As Balasaraswati was born into a family steeped in performing arts, not learning and not absorbing these age-old traditions was unimaginable. In fact, Balasaraswati's grandmother ran her house with an iron fist and no one was allowed to while away time. Even the children of the family were expected to devote and dedicate themselves to the constant practice of their art.

This tradition was followed so strictly that if Balasaraswati was playing on the streets she would be reprimanded and called upstairs to practice. There is an intriguing anecdote related to this. It was believed that even when Veenai Dhanammal had gone blind owing to her age, she could still sense if the kids were playing or practising just by hearing and figuring out which part of the house they were in. Not just this, if one tried to lie down or stretch one's legs she would know and the kids would be reprimanded.

One wonders whether it was this strict adherence to carrying on a rich legacy that robbed Balasaraswati of her childhood. Even as an adult, she was deeply in love with dolls. Any part of the world she travelled to, she would buy a doll from there. She might have been absorbing her family's art heritage through observation, but as Balasaraswati recalled in one of her interviews, she considered a madman to be her first guru.[4]

It so happened that when she was just a toddler, a beggar, who was almost a madman, used to visit their house begging for alms. He would, in all his craze, utter random dance phrases and Balasaraswati would be highly amused and dance along with the madman. It was later in life that she ruminated how that beggar could have been a divine ascetic who introduced her to dance and gave her his blessing to live an enchanted life of art. How else, she wondered, would he know that he had to sing and dance just when he came to their house despite no one in Balasaraswati's family being a dancer at that time.

∽

---

[4]Kumar, Sandhya, 'A Life That Was Art: The Dancer Balasaraswati', *Asia Society*, 24 June 2010, https://tinyurl.com/4vpw7pky. Accessed on 30 January 2023.

All of Balasaraswati's family was into music. Her grandmother; mother, Jayammal (who later accompanied her in dancing); her brothers, T. Ranganathan and T. Viswanathan, were all engrossed in the creation, rendition and teaching of music.

Balasaraswati was born at a time when popular societal norms were moving against entertainers and more so against dancers. In fact, her mother was worried that she might be ridiculed if she learnt dance. Although, Balasaraswati's ancestors did perform Sadir Attam[5], they never did so for the public. Her family danced only for the temples of their patron Mudaliar family.

Despite strong family resistance, even from Veenai Dhanammal, Balasaraswati's mother decided to train her in dance. She went ahead and found a young *nattuvanar*, the now revered, Kandappa Pillai. However, even before training with Guru Kandappa Pillai, Balasaraswati's young mind was captivated by the famed dancer, Mylapore Gauri Ammal, and all the craze of devadasi culture in those heady days that was slowly fading away.

Balasaraswati went on to admit that more than the revivalists, Mylapore Gauri Ammal should have been lauded for the preservation of Bharatanatyam. She was so fascinated by Gauri Ammal that whenever she visited her backstage after a concert, she would try on Ammal's anklets and dream of herself in a mythical and mystical (and more than anything—divine) world full of Gods and demons.

---

[5]Once a girl became a devadasi, she started training in the dance form called Sadir Attam also known as Dasi Attam. The name was done away with in 1950s, officially making it Bharatanatyam.

Before her mother and guru could commence her dance training, as was tradition in any performer's community, Balasaraswati had to be dedicated ritually to a temple. Although in the 1920s, the dedication of girls to temples was not unlawful, it was certainly looked down upon and often met with hostility.

Under such circumstances, the act of Balasaraswati's dedication to the Kamakshi temple in Thanjavur was carried out in 1922 by a devadasi, Rajayee Ammal. The ritual had to be wrapped in layers of secrecy. The items to be used in the rituals were disguised, the temple priest was sent away for an errand and the guards of the temple were bribed. With these preparations, Balasaraswati performed a small piece from her family's repertoire of dances in front of the Goddess Kamakshi (who was herself a manifestation of desire and blessed devotees with all that they desired).

Perhaps, Balasaraswati asked the Goddess to grant her the boon of becoming a dancer and her wish was truly granted. In later years, she proved instrumental in taking the regional performing art across the globe. Balasaraswati's dedication meant that now she was ready for a life of rigorous learning and practice of Bharatanatyam.

The gravity of the struggles she faced while learning from Kandappa Pillai were revealed in one of her interviews, years later. Balasaraswati had come to Delhi for recital. Maya Rao, then a disciple of Shambhu Maharaj, was scheduled to interview her. In that interaction, Maya Rao, with deep admiration, complimented Balasaraswati on her breathtaking style.

Any other artist would have smiled, nodded and moved on to the next question but Balasaraswati reproached the interviewer by asking her if she knew the level of training needed to achieve this mastery over a dance form. She then revealed a scar on her arm that Guru Kandappa Pillai had inflicted by burning her with a hot coal when she could not execute a certain movement. Then, during the interview itself she immediately broke into an impromptu *abhinaya* reminiscing her days as a student.[6]

After years of perfecting her dance, Balasaraswati's gurus and her family were ready for her *arangetram*, which is a debut recital by an artist where the guru presents their disciple to the public for the first time. As was the norm in those days, she had to perform the recital twice in one day.

The daytime viewing was reserved for women and the evening performance for the male members of the soirée. It is hardly any wonder that the young Balasaraswati passed with flying colours even under the intense scrutiny she had faced during both the performances.

Thus began her journey as an independent artist, ready to forge her way into the concert circuits and make her name. Balasaraswati was born at a time when the era of devadasis (and several other communities), women entertainers and performers was on the wane. Inspired by Abrahamic and Victorian sensibilities of modesty, an entire generation of Indians equipped with a western education were staunchly against these communities. Despite being a crucial part of the

---

[6]Knight, Douglas M., *Balasaraswati: Her Art and Life*, Wesleyan University Press, 2010.

fabric of civil society, artists have, since time immemorial, lived on the fringes of this so-called polite society.

Women artists have had to face double the wrath, since any woman who performed in front of men was considered to be of a loose moral character. With the arrival of the British who had little inclination towards understanding indigenous cultures, these sensibilities were heightened, despite the fact that these women were sophisticated and learned artists.

By the time Balasaraswati was ready to blossom into a full-blown artist, the Madras Legislative Council passed the Madras Devadasis (Prevention of Dedication) Act, just a few months after India's independence in 1947. This Act declared devadasis illegal. Among other repercussions, this also meant that the devadasi communities lost direct patronage of temples on which their livelihood depended. This Act proved to be the last nail in the coffin of women performers and their cause for a very long time. In Balasaraswati's case, it was a dry spell of five years before she could perform again in public.

∽

Contrary to the image of traditional performers being sexually promiscuous (which led to the abolishment of devadasis), Balasaraswati took on a companion at the age of 18 and remained faithful to him until his demise.

Her partner was R.K. Shanmukham, a prosperous entrepreneur who was the very first minister of finance in the cabinet of Jawaharlal Nehru. He was already married when he chose Balasaraswati as his life partner, a tradition that had little stigma at that time. Their partnership was further blessed by Balasaraswati's matrilineal clan and Shanmukham was a familiar sight in their residence.

Balasaraswati's association with Shanmukham, nevertheless, was not without conflict. As both were stalwarts in their respective fields; one was keen on declaring himself as an authority on the other's art while the other strived to maintain the independent spirit she was born with.

Apart from this, there were still other battles that Balasaraswati had to fight. She tried to restore traditional art to its previous status in the artistic and cultural structure of India. In a creative dispute, she took on the cult revivalist, Rukmini Devi Arundale to legitimize the credibility of *shringara rasa*, or the expression of love, which Arundale aimed to reconstitute.

While Balasaraswati was a direct successor of devadasis, as mentioned previously, her mother and grandmother had chosen to be musicians instead of dancers. This was due to the obvious moral objections that surrounded dance in that era. Rukmini Devi, on the other hand, hailed from an upper class Brahmin family and was tied in a marital union with English theosophist, George Arundale, at 16. This allowed her to have a more cosmopolitan lifestyle.

She even met Anna Pavlova, the famed ballerina, and was enchanted with her dance, soon beginning to learn from Pavlova's company dancer, Cleo Nordi. Pavlova inspired Rukmini Devi to explore her own roots and so she began learning dance in Tamil Nadu. Eventually, she founded the famed Kalakshetra Foundation in Madras, which had an enormous influence on the growth and dissemination of modern day Bharatanatyam.

As we can see, there were two performers existing in the same era (approximately). One emerged from within the lineage, while the other from beyond. One of them began dancing as a toddler, the other as an adult. Rukmini Devi believed that her purpose was to deliver dance from its depravity and that its distorted action language had to be purged. To restore its ancient morality, dance had to be brought under the safeguard of the 'honourable communities', namely the upper and middle class non-traditional families.

Balasaraswati, on the contrary, maintained that dance did not need to be filtered because it was not tainted in the first place. To quote Balasaraswati: 'There is nothing in Bharata Natyam which can be purified afresh; it is divine as it is and innately so. The shringara we experience in Bharata Natyam is never carnal; never, never. For those who have yielded themselves to its discipline with total dedication, dance like music is the practice of the Presence; it cannot be merely the body's rapture.'[7]

As per Balasaraswati, Rukmini Devi reinvented Bharatanatyam to represent contemporary Western theatre sensibilities and then, ultimately disassociated the new performers from the derogatory perceptions connected to the hereditary artists. It was as if Rukmini was attempting to suggest that a performance was self-contained and majestic; autonomous of the dancer's presentation and other stage props. In comparison to Rukmini Devi, Balasaraswati's outfits and set design were far less ostentatious.

---

[7]Balasaraswati, T., 'Bharata Natyam', *Sahapedia*, https://tinyurl.com/bdhrh5wy. Accessed on 30 January 2023.

For Balasaraswati, bhakti and shringara had no distinction. In her presidential address at the 33rd Annual Conference of the Tamil Isai Sangam held on 21 December 1975, she articulates with great depth how shringara for her is never carnal. Comparing the practice of dance to yogic sadhana, she states, 'For those who have yielded themselves to its discipline line with total dedication, dance, like music is the practice of the Presence. It cannot be merely the body's rapture.'[8] Balasaraswati notably drew an analogy of a divine sanctuary when explaining the nuanced shades of Bharatanatyam in her keynote.

Using the literary influence of the *Natyashastra*[9] and her own succinct experience, she reimagined the *margam*, establishing metaphysical comparisons among dance, temple architecture and sacred practice. Interestingly, several of Balasaraswati's most popular pieces associated with her throughout her lifetime—including 'Krishna Nee Begane Baaro', Vaarugalamo', Muktee Alikkum', 'Ka Va Va' and many other Tamil hymns—were non-sringara compositions.

However, their inclusion in her ensemble did not signify the dismissal of sringara rasa. These pieces simply reflected her artistic range and the versatility provided by her musical lineage. It is believed that once, in 1954, Balasaraswati visited the shrine of Lord Murugan in Thiruttani. So intense was her belief in the purity of art that she began to perform for the deity of Murugan after sending the priest away on an

---

[8] 'T Balasaraswati on Bharatanatyam', *Dancer's Paradise*, https://tinyurl.com/24ptz7pu. Accessed on 30 January 2023.
[9] Authored by Bharat Muni, it is an ancient comprehensive Sanskrit text on performing arts

undertaking and bribing the security guard. Balasaraswati, who at that point had begun to get sick, began to improve after her trip to Thiruttani. 'What dancing He worked through me, He alone knows,' she is said to have mentioned to her daughter, Lakshmi.[10]

The battle of reinstating her traditional art to its rightful status remained a lifelong one for Balasaraswati. Meanwhile, her destiny was conjuring up plans to put her on the limelight on an international stage.

∽

Astounded by Balasaraswati's quality of performance, the renowned dancer, Uday Shankar, orchestrated a Madras evening for her and subsequently persuaded her to appear in Calcutta at the All Bengal Music Conference in 1934. Balasaraswati appeared there, performing a song that would go on to become the national anthem of India. She gave a resounding performance of 'Jana Gana Mana' in the presence of Rabindranath Tagore himself. A year after that, Tagore was pleased to witness her work again at the All-India Music Conference in Banaras.

Balasaraswati's reputation extended far and wide in the Indian subcontinent. It was in the summer of 1961 that she made her first international trip to the East–West Music Encounter Convention held in Tokyo, Japan. A junior division official in the Ministry of Arts (then under the education ministry) argued, 'We can't send a fat, dark, tall

---

[10]Knight, Douglas M., *Balasaraswati: Her Art and Life*, Wesleyan University Press, 2010, p. 89.

woman dancer to Japan to represent India.'[11] She still went there and at the Metropolitan Concert Hall in Tokyo in 1961 she met Lord Harewood, a relative of Queen Elizabeth, who invited her to the prestigious Edinburgh Festival.

In 1962, the United States (US) press gave her performance a great review, once she made her debut at the famed Jacob's Pillow Dance Festival. While garlanding her after one of her performances, Ted Shawn quipped before the audience, 'Tonight you are in the presence of greatness.' [12]

From that day forward, it was almost like there wasn't a well-known dance conference that didn't include Balasaraswati's Bharatanatyam dance recital. She was, in fact, the first artist in her hereditary style of dance who presented it outside of South India. Balasaraswati, facilitated by the administration of the famed Music Academy in Chennai (then Madras), founded the Balasaraswati Institute of Performing Arts. There, realizing her dream, she successfully trained performers in Bharatanatyam, which was resplendent with shringara.

In the mid-1960s, she toured more and more internationally, appearing in East Asia, Europe and North America, which was fast becoming her second home. After that, mostly in mid-1970s and 1980s, she toured the US, extensively holding residencies—both as an educator and a dancer. Mills College (Oakland, California), California

[11]Khokar, Ashish Mohan, 'Ashish Khokar Salutes Bala', *The Hindu*, 8 February 2018, https://tinyurl.com/3ujnzpkj. Accessed on 30 January 2023.
[12]Sai, Veejay, 'Tanjore Balasaraswati: The Empress of Bharatanatyam', *Mint*, 17 June 2017, https://tinyurl.com/yr2cd9ja. Accessed on 30 January 2023.

Institute of Arts (Valencia), Washington University (Seattle), among many others were frequently visited by Balasaraswati.[13]

With her international presentations as well as her initiatives in India, particularly in Madras, Balasaraswati not only introduced myriad spectators to the classic fashion in which Bharatanatyam was rendered but also taught her dance style to numerous new students.

∽

> The testy dancer chides the singer, 'Don't whisper, sing!' The singer obediently raises her voice, but the dancer is still not satisfied. She launches into a melodic curve with a force of her own, to match the feeling she wishes to evoke, in both the music and dance. Is the singer annoyed? Not at all. Why, she is nodding her head in appreciation![14]

The dancer referred to above was Balasaraswati and the singer was the famous M.S. Subbulakshmi herself! Balasaraswati, with her childlike smile and innocence, drew friends, admirers and spectators from all walks of life. Her deep and lifelong friendship with music stalwart M.S. Subbulakshmi was one such treasured association. Back in those days, Subbulakshmi lived about three houses away from Balasaraswati's. These two artistic giants were members of the same devadasi

---

[13]'T. Balasaraswati', *Britannica.com*, https://tinyurl.com/2xyxn43t. Accessed on 30 January 2023.

[14]Ramnarayan, Gowri, 'Balasaraswati: In Whom Music and Dancing Merged', *DNA*, 31 December 2017, https://tinyurl.com/226x626s. Accessed on 30 January 2023.

family, and Balasaraswati had immense regard for what Subbulakshmi had achieved.

When once a year, Balasaraswati performed at the Music Academy, Subbulakshmi would always be in the front row. Balasaraswati often performed for events organized by the other, and even Subbulakshmi was there to lend her shoulder to Balasaraswati when her companion, R.K. Shanmukham passed away.

Balasaraswati was an artists' artist, from whom music and dance fused into a single character. It is widely known how Carnatic singers have come to *hear* her dance concerts. Hindustani singers have been enraptured by her too. The purist, Ustad Amir Khan, is said to have approached her to swap ragas and harmonic variations. They practised together for hours, deaf to the outside world. Ustad Vilayat Khan too treasured the warmest memories of the innocent Balasaraswati—performing as she did, letting Raag Bihag's romantic aroma float into the central courtyard of a Calcutta mansion.

She also enjoyed a wonderful relationship with other contemporaries in North India, whether they were dancers like Pandit Shambhu Maharaj or musicians like Pt Ravi Shankar. It was her angelic smile that besotted the famous film-maker Satyajit Ray to make a documentary on her life. Andrew Robinson, in his book, *Satyajit Ray: The Inner Eye*, mentions how Satyajit Ray became fascinated by Balasaraswati and also talks about the initial push for him to make the documentary:

Satyajit first saw Balasaraswati, 'the greatest Bharata Natyam dancer ever' according to him, in Calcutta in 1935. He was fourteen—just falling under the sway of western classical music—and she was about seventeen. He immediately fell for her. Ray was originally to have made his film [Bala] in 1966, when Bala was forty-eight. Something went wrong and he could not get started until 1976. He felt a twinge of regret at having missed recording her in her prime but consoled himself with the thought that Bala filmed at 58 was better than Bala not being filmed at all.[15]

We do not really witness a relaxed Balasaraswati in Ray's footage but rather an agitated one—striving to control her flowing locks and saree. We witness a performer attempting to react to musical notes and phrases emitting from an instrument that she couldn't see or communicate with.

There seems to be some poignant subtlety to all of this, since Balasaraswati often spoke about the artificial, consumerist representations of this sort that cut off the intrinsic ties between the performer and the music. A few critics also go on to claim that whatever is, therefore, retained in Ray's film and maintained as a gem in the Indian National Archives is a very mechanical rendition of Balasaraswati's greatness. Such dichotomy existed even when the artist was alive. The soirées she organized consisted only a handful of refined connoisseurs.

A reviewer once observed that Balasaraswati 'demonstrates how aesthetic pleasure and ethical instruction can be expressed simultaneously through music, dance and acting'.[16]

---

[15]Robinson, Andrew, *Satyajit Ray: The Inner Eye*, University of California Press, 1989.

[16]Ramnarayan, Gowri, 'Balasaraswati: In Whom Music and Dancing

Further, Clive Barnes, a dance critic, in a *New York Times* piece, has said: 'A dancer such as Bala makes nonsense of ethnic boundaries. Faced with an artist of the stature of this great bharatanatyam dancer, one looks and wonders, and salutes a great dancer when one sees her.'[17]

Just as the river mirrors leaves and flowers from arched trees, her voice flourished with the Hindustani musical blends she cherished, without veering away from her organic, time-worn course. Pandit Ravi Shankar has remarked about Balasaraswati:

'...I still remember what she played... I remember clearly that while listening to her, I had tears in my eyes.... She had something very special, apart from technique. There was so much feeling, soul and emotion; that could bring tears to people's eyes. This is what Bala herself inherited.'[18]

The West's recognition of Balasaraswati expanded the viewership of Indian performing arts, but only slightly. After all, knowing that Margot Fonteyn or Martha Graham were influenced by Balasaraswati mattered so little to Indians who barely understood these distant stars. However, neither Balasaraswati, nor the eight generations of talented artists in her household worried much about the validation of the public.

For Gauhar Jaan's visit to her place, Balasaraswati threw a lavish banquet in the 1920s costing over ₹1,000, with

Merged', *DNA*, 31 December 2017, https://tinyurl.com/226x626s. Accessed on 30 January 2023.

[17]Srinivasan, Sujata, 'Destined to Dance', *IndiaCurrents*, 24 February 2011, https://tinyurl.com/4tpymdwy. Accessed on 30 January 2023.

[18]Sai, Veejay, 'Tanjore Balasaraswati: The Empress of Bharatanatyam', *Mint*, 17 June 2017, https://tinyurl.com/yr2cd9ja. Accessed on 30 January 2023.

hospitality by the costliest British caterer, Harrison & Co.[19]

Her glorious family heritage was documented in the 1800s with Papammal (dancer) and her daughter Rukmini (vocalist) at the famed Thanjavur court. The parallel arts were inextricably nurtured by heirs to the impoverished Veenai Dhanammal (whose title ironically means riches). Nevertheless, Balasaraswati revealed sparkling jewels of a far more durable nature to those who endured the loud lanes of Georgetown in Old Madras to catch the Friday night soirees at her house.

Once asked why their style attracted so few audiences, her granddaughter Brinda responded, 'Not everyone is so lucky!' and her grandson Viswanathan concluded, 'And besides, a jeweller showcases his diamonds to the few who recognize its importance.'

Balasaraswati's family, including herself, saw themselves as the guardians of the high art they inherited and practised and did not let any notions of popular art sway their style. Later, it became a forte of Balasaraswati to represent the 'original' style of Bharatanatyam. She resisted the urge to cater her craft for a western audience. When she performed, movement translated to music; tune into a visual.

∽

Balasaraswati gained worldwide recognition while being in India and was bestowed with several awards. Outside of India, Balasaraswati was also featured in the coveted Dance

---

[19]Khokar, Ashish Mohan, 'Ashish Khokar Salutes Bala', *The Hindu*, 8 February 2018, https://tinyurl.com/3ujnzpkj. Accessed on 30 January 2023.

Heritage Coalition series called, 'America's Irreplaceable Dance Treasures: The First 100' (2000).[20]

In *The New York Times* (1977 review), dance critic, Anna Kisselgoff, defined her as being among the 'supreme performing artists in the world'. [21]

Visual artists and writers continue to exist through their work long after they are gone. But performers can only live on through their fans and disciples. Balasaraswati taught a few Indian and international pupils. However, she has also said, very frankly (according to many oral accounts), that she prefers if her work would perish with her. Even her own daughter, Lakshmi, had to assert her legitimate inheritance of dance only through osmosis.

Those who have seen Balasaraswati dancing at the height of her profession likened the sensation of glory to that elicited by the legendary 1,000-year-old temple of Brihadeeswara at Thanjavur.

Balasaraswati enjoyed her last years in her residence in Kilpauk, constructed with her hard-earned income. After a long, age-related illness, she died on 9 February 1984. Her identity is upheld by her disciples, and so she still lives on.

---

[20]'Balasaraswati, Indian Bharatanatyam Dancer', *IndiaNetzone*, 30 December 2011, https://tinyurl.com/5ycz4urf. Accessed on 30 January 2023.

[21]Sastry, Patruni Chidananda, 'Flag-Bearers of Indian Classical Dance', Medium, 8 March 2018, https://tinyurl.com/3hpfpd85. Accessed on 30 January 2023.

GLOSSARY

Abhinaya: Expressive approaches used to portray a topic, emotion or concept in Indian classical dance

Abhisarika Nayika: One of the eight archetypal states of the romantic heroine mentioned in *Natyashastra* as 'Ashta-Nayikas'. Abhisarika is the one who abandons her modesty and leaves her house to meet her beloved in secrecy.

Ada: Etiquette

Agamas: They are a compendium of the Hindu schools' tantric writings and texts

Alap: In a traditional North Indian classical presentation, the alap is the first segment. It is a type of melodic exploration of a raga that begins and ends with a crescendo.

Andaaz: Flair

Apsara: In Hindu and Buddhist traditions, an apsara is a feminine spirit of the sky and rivers. Apsaras are frequently depicted in art, dance, texts and folklore.

Arangetram: A Tamil word that refers to a student's first on-stage performance in Indian classical dance and music

Arya: Noble lady

Āshwamedha Yagna: The Ashwamedha was a Vedic horse offering ceremony practised by the Śrauta tradition of Vedic religion.

Awadh: Also known as Avadh or Oudh in colonial historical sources, it is a territory and planned state in modern-day Uttar Pradesh, India.

Baiji: A colonial term for courtesans belonging to the Bengal province

Baithak: A festive gathering to entertain company with music, dance and poetry

Begum: A title of aristocracy and royalty spanning central and south Asia

Bhava: It refers to a mood, feeling or devotional frame of consciousness in Indian classical dance.

Charkha: Spinning wheel used for cotton

Crorepati: A Hindi term for a millionaire

Dadra: A light classical vocal genre of the Hindustani classical music tradition

Darshan: An occasion to view or an event to see a sacred individual or a deity's manifestation

Devadasi: A temple courtesan belonging to South Indian states

Dhobi: Clothes cleaner

Dhrupad Dhamar: The oldest surviving genres of Hindustani or North Indian classical music

Diwan: A former princely Indian state's main treasury officer, minister of finance or prime minister

Durbars: Royal courts of Indian sovereigns

Dvija-Mukhyatama: He who knew the Vedas and scriptures and was a great warrior too

Fatwa: A recognized authority's decision on an issue of Islamic law

Ganga–Jamuna Tehzeeb: The culture of North India's central plains, which is a synthesis of Hindu and Muslim cultural and religious aspects.

Ganika: A category of courtesan in ancient India

Gaanewalis: Professional singers; usually referring to female singers

Gayaki: Singing style

Gayika: Female singers

Ghazal: A form of short poetry with Arabic origins, it has central themes of love and separation

Gopuram: It is a towering, decorative turret that stands at the gateway of most temples, notably in southern India, where Dravidian architectural style is prevalent.

Hafiza: A cult of courtesans belonging to the Kashmir region in the Indian subcontinent

Hakeem: Physician

Hammam: A communal bathhouse with Turkish origins

Haveli: Mansion

Jagir: A sort of feudal land grant in India's jagirdari (zamindari) system

Janpad Kalayani: Honorary title awarded to the prettiest maiden of the Janapada (kingdom)

Jatak Katha: A vast collection of Indian literature that details Gautam Buddha's former lives as both a man as well as an animal

Karshapanas: Ancient Indian coinage dating from the sixth century BCE onwards.

Khawasin: An Urdu term for attendant or handmaiden

Khayal: Throughout north India, this is a popular type of Hindustani classical music. Ragas are heavily embellished in khayal, and the form emphasizes technical skill above intellectual rigour.

Kharaj Bharan: Lower octave

Khuda: God

Kirtan: A devotioanl song in which a group repeats lines sing by a leader

Kotha: Residence of courtesans belonging to north Indian region

Kshatriya: This is one of Hindu culture's four staged varna system (social classes), and it is linked with military aristocracy

Kund: A holy pond

Lajja: Trepidation or shyness

Mahajanapadas: Between the sixth and fourth century BCE, 16 states or oligarchic republics flourished in ancient North India. These were known as Mahajanapadas.

Mahalsara: A Persian word for harem or female apartments

Mahari: A courtesan dedicated to the temples in erstwhile Orissa state

Malwa: A historical central region of Indian subcontinent situated amidst a volcanic plateau

Mara: Mara is the goddess of death in Hinduism

Margam: The linear structure practised by Bharatanatyam performers.

Mehfil: A gathering of people, usually connoisseurs of music. Alternatively, an evening of courtly entertainment, such as poetry or a performance.

Mrcchakatika: A Sanskrit 10-act play credited to Shudraka

Mridangist: Player of the mridangam, a barrel-shaped double-headed drum with one head larger than the other, used in South Indian music

Mugdha Nayika: A nayika or a heroine in her early teens who is naive and submissive

Mujra: A diluted form of entertainment that emerged from classical Kathak

Mutah: In Islamic law, it is temporary matrimony or is a personal and verbal transient marriage arrangement; metaphorically, a 'pleasure marriage'.

Nagarvadhu: The most attractive lady as well as the most skilful in different dance styles was appointed as the Nagarvadhu, literally translating to 'the bride of the town', in some areas of ancient India.

Nanand: Sister-in-law

Narmada: A holy river in central India

Nattuvanar: Traditionally, the Nattuvanar was the guru and the choreographer and also the one who wielded the cymbals.

Natyachar: A dance teacher in ancient India

Nautch: Courtly dances in later Mughal and early British Raj era

Nayaka: Male protagonist

Nayika: Female protagonist

Nikah: A marriage by Islamic law

Nitya Sumangali: Devadasis or temple dancers married to the presiding deity were considered forever married women because their husband, being God, could never die.

Nazrana: Fee

Pakka Gana: A pre-Independence era colloquial term for Indian classical music

Purab Ang: Musical traditions like thumri that were affected by the Awadhi style of singing

Raga: It is a melodic underpinning for experimentation, similar to Indian classical music's harmonic mode

Ragadaari: The art of elaborating the patterns of any particular raga

Rajanartiki: A royal court dancer from ancient to medieval India

Rang Pravesham: A debut recital of any performing artist male or female

Rudb: Dignity, or power of commanding personal respect

Sadir Attam: A precursor of Bharatanatyam, it was a parlour or salon style of dance practised by the courtesans of South India between fourteenth to nineteenth century

Satlarha: A pearl necklace with seven strings

Sarai: A medieval era resting place; a caravan station where travellers would rest

Sarangi: A string instrument from North India

Sati: It was a Hindu tradition in which a widow perched atop her departed partner's funeral pyre to die along with him. It is now archaic.

Shauhar: Husband

Sepoy: Indian soldiers

Swadeshi: Literally translates to 'of one's own country'

Taleem: Education

Talkie: A colloquial term for a movie

Tawaifs: A courtly entertainer from North Indian region highly sophisticated in the arts of music, dance and poetry

Thumri: Musical tradition with bhakti or romantic themes in parlances of Hindi called Awadhi and Brij

Ujjaiyini: Ancient name of the present city of Ujjain, which was the capital of Gupta dynasty during Indian classical era

Ustad: An Urdu term for master or Guru

Viraha: A Sanskrit term for the pain of separation from ones' beloved

Walima: Marriage reception

Zardosi: It is an Iranian needlework style that incorporates pearls, jewels, precious stones and is made with gold and silver strands.

Zenana: A female seraglio in the Muslim, Sikh or Hindu aristocracies

ACKNOWLEDGEMENTS

Destiny plays a strange part in one's life. Being an ever-inquisitive and fidgety Indian classical dancer, I am always curious about what can be and, more so, about what was. In my unending pursuit to find connections between the glorious tales of the past and the world of performing arts in the present, I tend to keep digging, to the exasperation of my gurus and senior scholars.

I have had a curious mind since childhood. I went from wondering if I could dance to becoming a professional by questioning why we need the arts; what 'classical' means; how classical arts are relevant in this fast-paced, modern world; and, most importantly, where do I, a male practitioner of a 2,000-year-old Odissi dance tradition, fit into it all? In this quest for answers, over years of research, I came across terms like 'devadasi', 'rajadasi', 'narthaki', 'ganika', 'tawaif', 'nautch girls' and, of course, 'courtesan' quite early on. The deeper I delved into their stories, the more enchanted I became with this world.

Then one day, my phone rang and on the other end was a sweet voice asking me, 'Is this Madhur Gupta?' This turned out to be of my soon-to-be editor, Saswati Bora, from Rupa Publications, asking me to author a book on the topic of women entertainers and performers of India. Not only did I find myself in extremely familiar territory but also marvelled at how destiny keeps pushing me to achieve my life's objective—to create beauty! I am ever so grateful to Saswati for being exceptionally patient with a slow writer like me, continually guiding, editing and discussing the shape our book should take.

Had it not been for my parents, the late Dr Usha Gupta and Isht Deo Gupta, who gave me the freedom to be whatever I dreamed of, I would never have had the confidence to forge my path into the sublime sphere of classical arts. Although my mother passed away over a decade ago, her words still ring in my ear, pushing me to not settle for anything less: 'Be what you want to be, but be on your own time and money and be the best at it!' My father sent me to train in the classical arts under the able guidance of Pandit Birju Maharaj from a very early age. Although I never performed Kathak as a professional, the time I spent with Maharaj ji helped shape my young mind with the rich history of Indian performing arts and showed me how classical arts are like a river that refreshes itself as it flows from one ghat to the other.

Destiny again chose Odissi dance for me when I accidentally joined an introductory workshop conducted by my first guru of Odissi, Madhavi Mudgal. She sowed the seed of love for the ancient dance form in me. In my quest to delve deeper into the culture, I chose to spend a few years in Orissa under Guru Bichitranand Swain, fondly known as Bichi Sir. He rooted me firmly in this art form and gave me the gravitas to continue on the path to perfect it. Currently, Guru Sharon Lowen ji's able guidance is helping me reach the deeper recesses of an unending artistic journey. In this process, she has been the lilting branches and fragrant flowers without which the graceful soul of my art would have remained elusive. I offer this book as a small literary homage at my gurus' feet.

I am deeply grateful to my family and friends, Shikha di, Neha di, Shreya, Shonik, Radhika, Payal and my Luna who motivated me through moments of self-doubt. I am thankful to my brilliant disciples with whom I get to have some of the most intellectual discussions on the relevance of art practices and their future.

My heartfelt thanks to Shashi Tharoor, Mallika Sarabhai, Ustad Zakir Hussain, Anoushka Shankar, Zubin Mehta and Pandit Birju Maharaj ji for supporting my endeavour to bring to light the fabulous lives of these incredible women of courage, beauty and art. I am grateful to all the scholars and authors whose work inspired me to write this book in so many intangibly valuable ways.

Last but not the least, I am most thankful to everyone at Rupa Publications for bringing artists like me, who mostly remain aloof and on the fringes of society, into the mainstream.

BIBLIOGRAPHY

Ahmad, Muhammad Taqi, *Begums of Oudh: History in the Making*, Shubhi Publications, 1 January 2021.

Bapat, P.V. (ed.), *2500 Years of Buddhism*, The Publications Division, Ministry of Information and Broadcasting, Government of India, 1956.

Chandra, Moti, *The World of Courtesans*, Vikas Publishing House Pvt Ltd, 1973.

Desai, Kishwar, *Darlingji: The True Love Story of Nargis and Sunil Dutt*, HarperCollins India, 2007.

Ejaz, A.D. (ed.), *Rani Roopmati*, Ratan and Co-Book Sellers, Delhi.

Fraser, James Baillie, *Military Memoir of Lieut.-Col. James Skinner*, Cambridge University Press, 2012.

Ganguly, Rita, and Sabharwal, Jyoti, *Ae Mohabbat -- Reminiscing Begum Akhtar*, Stellar Publishers, 2008.

George, T.J.S., *The Life and Times of Nargis*, Westland, 2007.

Gupta, Archana Garodia, *The Women Who Ruled India: Leaders. Warriors. Icons.*, Hachette India, 2019.

Gupta, Dipankar (ed.), *Caste in Question: Identity or Hierarchy?*, SAGE Publications, 2004, p. 199.

Hirakawa, Akira, *A History of Indian Buddhism: From Śākyamuni to Early Mahāyāna*, Motilal Banarsidass, 1993.

Hiranand, Shanti, *Begum Akhtar: The Story of My Ammi*, Viva Books, 2005.

Kannabiran, Kalpana, 'Judiciary, Social Reform and Debate on "Religious Prostitution" in Colonial India', *Economic and Political Weekly*, Vol. 30, No. 43, 1995.

Kersenboom, Saskia C., *Nityasumaṅgalī: Devadasi Tradition in South India*, Motilal Banarsidass, 2016.

Knight, Douglas M., *Balasaraswati: Her Art and Life*, Wesleyan University Press, 2010.

Lall, John, *Begum Samru: Fading Portrait in a Gilded Frame*, Roli Books, 2012.

Larneuil, Michel, *Begum Samru of Sardhana*, Translated by Ranjit Sinha, Sahitya Akademi, 2011.

Levine, Philippa (ed.), *Gender and Empire*, Oxford University Press, 2007, pp. 134–55.

Levine, Philippa, 'A Multitude of Unchaste Women: Prostitution in the British Empire', *Journal of Women's History*, Johns Hopkins University Press, Vol. 15, No. 4, 2004, pp. 159–63.

Liddle, Swapna, *Chandni Chowk: The Mughal City of Old Delhi*, Speaking Tiger, 2017.

Llewellyn-Jones, Rosie, *The Last King in India: Wajid Ali Shah: Wajid Ali Shah, 1822-1887*, Hurst, 2014.

Mourad, Kenizé, *In the City of Gold and Silver: The Story of Begum Hazrat Mahal*, Full Circle, 2013.

Mukherjee, Debashree, *Bombay Hustle: Making Movies in a Colonial City*, Columbia University Press, 2020.

Mukherjee, Rudrangshu, *A Begum and A Rani: Hazrat Mahal and Lakshmibai in 1857*, Penguin Random House, 2021.

Mukherjee, Rudrangshu, *Awadh in Revolt, 1857-1858: A Study of Popular Resistance*, Anthem, 2002.

Mukherjee, Sutapa, *Begum Akhtar: The Queen of Ghazal*, Rupa & Company, 2003.

Nevile, Pran, *Nautch Girls of the Raj*, Penguin Books, 2009.

Oldenburg, Veena Talwar (ed.), *Shaam-E-Awadh: Writings on Lucknow*, Penguin Books, 2007.

Oldenburg, Veena Talwar, 'Lifestyle as Resistance: The Case of the Courtesans of Lucknow, India', *Feminist Studies*, Vol. 16, No. 2, 1990, pp. 259–87.

Rao, Shruthi, *10 Indian Women Who Were the First to Do What They Did*, Penguin Random House, 2019.

Robinson, Andrew, *Satyajit Ray: The Inner Eye*, University of California Press, 1989.

Ruswa, Mirza Muhammad Hadi, *Umrao Jan Ada: The Courtesan of Lucknow*, Translated by Khushwant Singh and M.A. Husaini, Orient Paperbacks, 1970.

Sampath, Vikram, *My Name is Gauhar Jaan: The Life and Times of a Musician*, Rupa Publications, 2012.

Samson, Leela, *Rukmini Devi: A Life*, Penguin Books, 2010.

Saran Gour, Neelam, *Requiem in Raga Janki*, Penguin Random House, 2018.

Sayed, Hares, *War, Violence, Terrorism, and Our Present World: A Timeline of Modern Politics*, Xilbris, 2017.

Shah, Vidya, *Jalsa: Women and Their Journeys from the Salon to the Studio*, Tulika Books, 2016.

Sharma, Mahindra Narain, *The Life and Times of Begam Samru of Sardhana [A.D. 1750–1836]*, Vibhu Prakashan, 1985.

Śūdraka, *The Clay Toy-Cart*, Translated by Rajappa Padmini, Penguin Random House, 2018.

Tiwari, Chandra Kant, 'Rupmati: "The Melody Queen of Malwa"', *Proceedings of the Indian History Congress*, Vol. 38, 1977, pp. 244–9.

Umari, Ahmad Ul, *The Lady of the Lotus*, Creative Media Partners, LLC., 2018.

Verma Ojha, Sumedha, *Urnabhih: A Mauryan Tale of Espionage, Adventure and Seduction*, Roli Books, 2014.

Vishwanathan, Lakshmi, *Women of Pride: The Devadasi Heritage*, Roli Books, 2008.